Women To Remember

Women To Remember

NATHANAEL OLSON

Portraits of
women who
helped shape
America

GOOD NEWS PUBLISHERS
Westchester, Illinois

This book,
a tribute to great American women,
is lovingly dedicated to:

Shirley, my devoted wife,
Melody and Joy, my delightful daughters,
Olive Olson, my loving mother,
Dorothy Bagley, my loyal mother-in-law—
the five great American ladies in my life!

Wauwatosa, Wisconsin
Mother's Day, 1976

Contents

Introduction

   Many women have written their lives big on the pages of
American history. All could not be included in this book.
Those selected reveal courage, faith, self-sacrifice,
compassion, vision, adventure and discipline in the fields of
education, culture, science, medicine, philanthropy and
government.

   With hands, heart and head godly women wrote books that
stirred two continents to end slavery, fought and won higher
education and the vote for women, opportunity in medicine,
destroyed racial barriers with the gift of song, reached youth
with a life-changing message. Often maligned and
unrewarded they chose to give America lives that helped
shape our destinies for good.

   In remembering these women who were not self-serving, in
recalling the continent-embracing results of their vision and
goals, lives are enriched and minds stretched to recognize
horizons of opportunity and problems of both spiritual and
material inequity. I invite you to meet women who made good
history out of hard times.

Muriel Dennis

Laura Ingalls Wilder

Author of *The Little House on the Prairie*

CHAPTER ONE

Mrs. Laura Wilder sighed wearily as she started to open the fat envelope which had just arrived in the morning mail. She knew what would be inside, her manuscript along with a rejection slip from the publisher.

This scene had been happening repeatedly ever since she had sent off her autobiography, which her daughter Rose had urged her to write. Titled *Little House in the Big Woods,* it was the story of Laura and her family, a story she knew well. It pulsated with adventure, romance, hardship, all ingredients of a good story. Yet no publisher would take it. What was wrong?

Finally, Laura wisely concluded that her story might be more for children than adults. She rewrote it, using more simple words and phrases. Then she mailed it to the children's editor at Harper and Brothers. Within three days, it was accepted.

Laura was born February 7, 1867, in a log cabin in Wisconsin, miles from the nearest town. Pioneers in the truest sense, the Ingalls, Pa, Ma, Laura, Mary and Baby Carrie, managed to live in the wilderness by raising their own vegetables, hunting deer and fowl and protecting themselves from bears, wolves and wildcats. And, of course, they had fun times together too, especially at Christmas time. When Laura was five, she received her first rag doll, so much more lifelike than the corncob doll she had been rocking to sleep!

11

Time passed and one day Pa decided to move. Too many settlers were coming into the Big Woods to suit him! The Ingalls put their few possessions into a covered wagon and traveled to Indian Territory, now the border of Oklahoma and Kansas. There Pa built the little house on the prairie and a barn beside it. He also dug a well.

After all their work, the government informed them that their homesite was reserved for Indians and that settlers would not be allowed to stay. Once more the covered wagon carried the Ingalls' belongings to a new destination, this time northward to Minnesota on the banks of Plum Creek.

During their last summer at Plum Creek, scarlet fever struck the family and as a result, Mary lost her sight. Faced with the new challenge of a blind daughter, Pa had no immediate solution.

A short time later, Pa moved his family farther west, helping to found the little town of De Smet, South Dakota. It was here that the Ingalls experienced the long hard winter, as Laura later titled her book. During the winter even the mercury in the thermometer froze! During these days of forty below zero weather when snow piled up to the second floor of the houses, the residents would have starved if two boys, Almanzo Wilder and Cap Garland, hadn't ridden forty miles to get some wheat from a farmer! Mercifully, Spring came at last, bringing new warmth and healing memories of the long, hard winter.

The following Fall, Mary began attending a school for the blind in Iowa where she learned to read and write in Braille.

Later Laura, who earned her teacher's certificate, went to work and helped to pay Mary's tuition. She also found time to be with Almanzo Wilder, one of the two boys who had saved their lives. In 1885, Almanzo and Laura were married and moved to the little gray house in the west.

The seven *Little House* books conclude with Laura's marriage, followed by *Farmer Boy*, the story of Almanzo's childhood in New York State.

12

Life, however, had many more experiences to offer the newly married couple. For three successive years, drought ruined their crops. In 1891, the little gray house burned to the ground. Later, the Wilders came down with diptheria which killed their son. Then Almanzo suffered a stroke and Laura worked in a dressmaker's shop twelve hours a day to earn a dollar.

In 1894, accompanied by their daughter Rose, Mr. and Mrs. Wilder moved south to Mansfield, Missouri. Here they established a dairy and poultry farm. Along with her flourishing farm work, Laura started enjoying success as a writer and editor. She was fifty-five years old, however, before her first *Little House* book was published.

She lived many years after this event, passing away at the age of ninety on February 10, 1957. Yet, through television her influence continues to increase. Today viewers of *Little House on the Prairie* continue to discover the wholesome, action-filled books of Laura Ingalls Wilder and a history of one of America's pioneer families!

Marian Anderson

The World's Greatest Contralto

CHAPTER TWO

If music had not been such an integral part of her being, Marian Anderson might have achieved her childhood ambition of being a surgeon. As a child she constantly bandaged and rebandaged her dolls. Whenever she attended the Union Baptist Church with her parents, however, and heard the spirited singing of Christians, she knew her own soul was bursting with song.

Soon she enrolled in her church's junior choir. A short time later, the choir director asked six-year-old Marian to blend her voice with that of a friend's. They sang the duet "Dear to the Heart of the Shepherd" for a church service. Her singing career had begun!

Born in Philadelphia in 1908, Marian quickly discovered the problems poverty brings. Both of her parents had to work hard and long. Her father delivered coal, wood, and ice; her mother worked domestic jobs. Sensing their daughter's fascination with the piano, Mr. and Mrs. Anderson determined to buy a second-hand one for her. When it arrived, the neighborhood children tingled with excitement, yelling, "The Andersons' piano is here!"

Marian had one problem, however; she had no funds to pay a piano teacher. Undaunted, she found a card which told the name of each note and inserted it behind the keys. With this bit of help, she learned to play simple accompaniments.

After hearing the rich notes of a violin, Marian set out to purchase her own instrument. Diligently scrubbing doorsteps and running errands for neighbors, she saved each coin. Finally she had the sum needed to buy the violin she had spotted in a pawn shop and proudly purchased the $3.98 instrument while an older cousin watched!

When Marian was ten, her father suffered a head injury which caused his death shortly after Christmas. With only one paycheck, her mother had to give up her small home and move herself and three daughters into Grandmother Anderson's large house, already overflowing with two cousins, an aunt and a number of day-care children. Marian's

15

mother, grateful and hard-working, took in laundry and traveled to homes needing domestic services.

Marian naturally wanted to help supplement the family's budget. Although she had no desire to be a stenographer, she thought it wise to enroll in a commercial course being offered at William Penn High School. The principal, however, recommended that she transfer into the music program at South Philadelphia High School. "I heard you sing in our assembly program," the principal said kindly, "and I feel you deserve the best musical training available."

Encouraged, Marian changed schools and concentrated on developing her God-given voice. Now a member of the senior choir at church, she delighted in memorizing all four parts of each anthem. With this extra preparation she could take any part, even bass, should a soloist be unable to be present.

At the annual music concert at Union Baptist Church, featured soloist Roland Hayes heard Marian sing. Impressed by her voice, he offered suggestions for the development of her singing career and later used his influence to open engagements for her in other areas besides Philadelphia.

Conscious of her need for further training, at the beginning of the term Marian went to a school of music to inquire about tuition costs. Students, shuffling their feet, stood in line waiting to register. Marian took her place and eventually reached the registration desk. The young employee ignored her and handed a registration form to the next person in line. Finally, when all the other students were helped, the employee turned to Marian. "Now, what do you want?" Marian replied that she merely wanted to know the cost of tuition. "We don't take colored," she snapped, turning to leave. The rebuff pierced Marian's sensitive soul and she stumbled out of the conservatory in tears. How cruel could prejudice be? How many others would reject her talent because of her racial background?

Discouraged but not defeated, she continued singing in churches, schools, and YMCA's. Sometimes she received

16

nothing but applause; other times she earned two dollars per performance. Finally as her fame began to spread, she dared ask a minimum fee of five dollars.

Near the time for her high school graduation, Principal Lucy Wilson volunteered to take Marian to audition for Giuseppe Boghetti, a master voice teacher who had a waiting list of students. After hearing her sing, he gruffly announced that he would immediately make room for her in his schedule. Then he stated his high fee, and Marian's mind reeled.

"I could never afford that much," she told Dr. Wilson as they walked away. "All I have is the money I manage to earn through singing." Dr. Wilson listened, wishing she knew some way to solve the dilemma.

Neither one of them, though, had figured on the love and loyalty of Marian's church friends. They began the "Fund for Marian Anderson's Future" and raised five hundred dollars through benefit concerts and church auxiliaries. Then, at graduation time, the Philadelphia Choral Society presented her with a scholarship. Later, the National Association of Negro Musicians provided a fund so that Marian could continue her lessons. Her dreams were coming true after all!

Boghetti proved to be a kind but firm teacher. He mixed in his solid philosophy of success with instructions on breathing and placement of tones. "You must learn to do your job under any circumstances," he told Marian. "You can never say, 'Tonight I don't feel well and I won't appear.'"

He helped her to plan her first professional program, a recital at Town Hall in New York. The concert proved to be a miserable failure for Marian, her friends and her sponsors. Afterwards, she told her mother, "I'd better forget all about singing." Her mother replied, "Pray about it, Marian."

Her daughter neglected to follow this wise counsel and for weeks succumbed to doubt, feelings of inferiority and despair. She turned down offers for concerts and even neglected her lessons at Boghetti's studio. Finally, her cycle of

17

despondency ended. Convinced that happiness and satisfaction would come only as she used her voice for God, Marian informed her mother, "I want to study again ... to be the best and be loved by everyone."

This decisiveness marked the beginning of a new life and a greater career for Marian. One success followed another. In 1923, she won a contest for soloists sponsored by the Philadelphia Philharmonic Society. In 1925, she entered another contest, this one sponsored by the Lewishohn Stadium concerts. One of sixteen chosen for the semifinals, Marian waited for further word at Mr. Boghetti's studio. Suddenly the telephone rang and her teacher grabbed it. He listened for a few moments and then exclaimed to his student, "There will be no finals! We have won!"

On August 26, 1925, Marian presented in her concert at the Lewishohn Stadium a delightful blending of spirituals and classics, such as "O Mio Fernando" from Donizetti's *La Favorita*. Impressed with the natural beauty of her voice and the dramatic way she projected each song, critics gave her good reviews. After this success, Marian's concert bookings increased as did her fees.

Although thankful for her growing fame, financial success meant more to Marian than merely a bulging bank account. When a reporter asked her "What was the greatest moment in your life?" she quickly responded, "The day I went home and told my mother that she wouldn't have to work any more."

Obviously, Marian's life contained other great moments. While on a concert tour of the Scandinavian countries, she was invited to the villa of the great Finnish composer, Jean Sibelius. After singing several songs for him, including one of his compositions, Sibelius exclaimed, "My roof is too low for you!" She also had the opportunity to sing before King Gustav in Stockholm and King Christian in Copenhagen.

At a private recital in Salzburg in 1935, Marian saw the brilliant conductor Toscanini in the audience. Her heart fluttered, wondering if she could please the demanding perfectionist. She sighed with relief when he came forward to congratulate her with these words: "Yours is a voice such as one hears once in a hundred years." Warmed by his gracious words, Marian enthusiastically finished her European concerts and embarked for her homeland and an appearance at New York City's Town Hall.

Aboard ship, the sea became rough. Marian slipped, and as she fell her ankle buckled under her. After her arrival in America, x-rays revealed that she had broken her ankle. The doctor then ordered her ankle placed in a cast for the next six weeks. "Six weeks?" she thought to herself, "and what about my December 30th concert at Town Hall?" Slowly and surely she planned her strategy.

On December 30, 1935, friends wheeled her on stage behind closed curtains. Then, giving her crutches to a friend, she leaned on the curve of the grand piano and struck a relaxed pose. Her long white dress hid the cast completely. When the curtains opened, she poured forth such golden tones that her audience, lifted to such musical heights, never had the time or desire to question her motionless stance.

Remembering the unflattering statements critics had made after her first performance in Town Hall many years before, Marian waited anxiously for the reviews in the morning papers. She had nothing to fear. "Grandeur of interpretation," wrote one. "She has returned to her native land one of the greatest singers of our time," exclaimed another.

19

Marian's future, however, was not to be trouble free. The prejudice thrust at her when she inquired about tuition at the conservatory appeared again, on a larger scale. In 1939, Marian's manager, the successful Sol Hurok, had tried to book her for a concert at Constitution Hall in Washington, D.C., owned by the Daughters of the American Revolution. But the owners ruled that a person of the Negro race could not appear on its stage!

This decision triggered emotional reactions from all levels

of society. Eleanor Roosevelt, America's First Lady, protested such bigotry by resigning from the Daughters of the American Revolution. Harold L. Ickes, Secretary of the Interior, invited Marian Anderson to sing in the open air from the Lincoln Memorial on Easter Sunday. After Marian had agreed, Sol Hurok advertised the event as a free concert for people who love music and believe in democracy for everyone. Seventy-five thousand people came!

Visibly moved by the love and concern of the crowd stretched in a great semicircle, Marian Anderson sang with all her being. In the spirituals, her audience heard the feelings of the oppressed; in her patriotic numbers, the crowd sensed the spiritual heritage that makes America great. After her closing number, tumultuous cheers pierced the atmosphere surrounding the Lincoln Memorial. It was, indeed, a fitting setting for a renewal of faith and freedom.

In 1939, Marian was chosen to be the recipient of the Springarn Medal, an award given annually to the American Negro who "shall have made the highest achievement ... in any honorable field of endeavor."

Two years later, in 1941, Marian was presented with the Bok Award, a ten thousand dollar prize given annually to "an outstanding citizen of Philadelphia." She channeled this money into a scholarship program to help young people pursue an artistic career. Neither race, creed, or color are considered in the granting of these scholarships.

As the initial scholarship fund diminished, Marian added her own personal money and established the Marian Anderson Scholarship. From this fund, many young singers have received financial assistance needed to reach their educational and artistic goals.

Marian has not forgotten the days when fame and fortune eluded her. She is grateful to God and to others for her successes such as her contract in 1954 with the Metropolitan Opera Company to sing the role of Ulrica in Verdi's *A Masked Ball;* being sent by the U.S. State Department on a goodwill mission to the Far East in 1957; her 1958 appointment by President Eisenhower as Alternate Delegate in the United States Mission to the United Nations.

Perhaps her greatest triumph, though, has been in her personal life. She is happily married to architect Orpheus Fisher, the boyfriend of her teen years. She neither drinks nor smokes, and refuses to fight hate with hate. "Things like fear and hate destroy you, restrict you from being the kind of big person you should be," Marian told a group of schoolboys in Lumpur.

At the center of these admirable qualities is her sincere and personal faith in God. The spiritual "He Has the Whole World in His Hands" is one of her favorites because it expresses the assurance she feels that the Lord is directing her life and career. "There was a time when I was very much interested in applause and the lovely things they said," Marian remembers. "But now we are interested in singing so that somebody in the audience will leave feeling a little better than when he came."

After her Houston concert, the *Texas Post* reported, "If there was a dry eye in the house it was because they sold a seat to a stone man." Consistently, Marian can "turn a concert hall into a temple," according to one admirer.

Such unsolicited praise reveals Marian Anderson to be more than a great singer; she is, in every sense of the word, a great woman. Perhaps Fannie Hurst summed it up best when she described Marian as someone who has "not grown simply great" but "has grown great simply."

Fanny Crosby

Prolific Blind Author of Favorite Hymns

CHAPTER THREE

Early in life, Fanny J. Crosby determined that if she had to be handicapped, it would be physically, not emotionally. As an eight-year-old, she penned eight lines which were to reflect her positive attitude during her long life of nearly ninety-five years:

"Oh, what a happy soul am I!
Although I cannot see,
I am resolved that in this world
Contented I will be.

How many blessings I enjoy
That other people don't;
To weep and sigh because I'm blind
I cannot, and I won't!"

When she wrote this bit of rhyme and meter, she had no way of knowing that someday her hymn poems would be sung around the world, making her one of the most beloved poets of all time.

Born March 24, 1820, in a rural cottage in Putnam County, New York, Frances Jane Crosby was only six weeks old when she lost her sight. A hot poultice, prescribed for eye infection, robbed her vision.

Before Fanny was a year old, her family suffered another loss when her father died. Forced to get a job, her mother went to work and her grandmother came to the little cottage to care for the blind baby.

23

With the passing years, Fanny and her grandmother became inseparable. Through Grandma's vivid pictures, Fanny began to "see" the world around her. Her growing imagination soon brought sunrise and sunset, stars and clouds into sharp focus. Her hearing enabled her to know whether the feathered friend in the nearest tree was a meadow lark or a whippoorwill.

Of course Grandmother took great pride in Fanny's

accomplishments, but sometimes became alarmed when Fanny courageously walked the top rail of fences. Fanny also learned to ride horseback.

Her most lasting accomplishments, however, were in the mental and spiritual areas of life. When her mother told her that some blind people had become some of the world's greatest poets, Fanny took an even greater interest in poetry and memorized John Milton's poem about his blindness.

Unwilling to lose the knowledge and appreciation for the Bible she had received as a young girl, she memorized the complete book of Ruth and passages from Psalms, Proverbs and the New Testament.

One day, she wrote:

> "O Book, that with reverence I honor,
> What joy in thy pages I see!
> O Book of my childhood devotion,
> More precious than rubies to me."

As Fanny began to experience a mental and spiritual awakening, she had a strong desire to be able to read for herself. She yearned to attend a school for the blind where she would be taught Braille, but had no idea how her mother would be able to secure the funds necessary for her tuition.

Fanny decided to pray about it and asked God to help her mother find some way to finance the tuition. Time passed. There seemed to be no solution. Yet, Fanny kept believing, desiring and, most important of all, praying.

The miracle happened. One morning at breakfast her mother announced, "Fanny, you can start getting your things together. God has made it possible for me to send you to the New York Institute for the Blind!"

Overjoyed, Fanny clapped her hands, and exclaimed, "Thank You, Lord, for answering my prayer!"

Soon the fourteen-year-old poet was in bustling New York City, a sharp contrast to her former world of whippoorwills and meadow larks. But she adjusted easily to life in the big city. She enjoyed studying with other determined young people who wouldn't allow blindness to frustrate their educational plans. Fanny did have one problem at school that she could not avoid. Her teachers frowned on her obsession with poetry. "You spend far too much time on this fanciful subject," they would say sternly. "You must take a greater interest in other areas of thought."

Wanting to please her instructors, Fanny tried to forget her poetry and turned her attention to other matters. But try as she might, she could not forget the music of words and phrases that came uninvited into her mind and heart. She *had* to write them down.

Finally, the tide turned in her favor. A noted doctor from Boston told her instructors, "Encourage this young poet all you can. Read the finest books of poetry to her. Someday you will hear from this young lady."

Fortunately for history, her teachers accepted his advice. Assured of support and understanding, Fanny began to write with even greater enthusiasm and her fame began to grow.

She became well known for her public recitations of poems, usually original ones. In 1842, Fanny joined a poetry group of twenty New York Institute students. They traveled by canal boat down the Hudson River, stopping to perform publicly in various towns along the way. Often the highlight of the program was the presentation of a new poem from the heart and lips of Fanny Crosby.

She had other interesting experiences. On one occasion, she met James K. Polk, the eleventh President of the United States. She also came in contact with William Cullen Bryant, Horace Greeley, Henry Clay and other notable men of her time. Before he became the President of the United States, Grover Cleveland served at the Institute and Fanny became his friend. This friendship continued even after he moved to the White House.

After twelve happy years of study it was easy for Fanny to

accept an offer to remain at the Institute and teach English grammar, rhetoric and ancient history. She taught her blind students for eleven years. They flocked around the cheerful, patient, empathetic, encouraging blind woman.

Teaching, however, did not fully express the creative flow of Fanny's mind and spirit. Writing seemed to be the best outlet. In 1844, her first volume of poetry, *The Blind Girl and Other Poems,* was published. Over twenty years later, she began writing hymn poems for William B. Bradbury, the composer of such beloved hymns as "Jesus Loves Me" and "Just As I Am."

In hymn writing, Fanny J. Crosby found her lifelong work. Estimates of her total output range from 5,500 to 9,000 poems. She often used pseudonymns, so it is virtually impossible to correctly number all her "brain children."

Her pattern of inspiration varied. Sometimes she wrote the words first and the composers had to wed her words to their melodies. Other times, she would hear a new tune and the melodic flow suggested a certain thought, such as "Safe In the Arms of Jesus" and "Blessed Assurance."

The latter hymn was written in the home of Mrs. Joseph Knapp, a wealthy woman in New York City who played an original composition for Fanny and then asked, "What does the melody line say to you, Fanny?"

The blind poet smiled. "That tune," she replied, "says 'Blessed assurance, Jesus is mine!' " In a short time, she wrote the song "Blessed Assurance" (which is a perennial favorite of millions) in the home of one of the founders of the Metropolitan Life Insurance Company.

As years passed and people sang her hymns around the world, Fanny would hear how God has used them in people's lives. For example, a missionary on furlough told her of meeting a little blind girl in Korea whom friends had nicknamed, "Little Blind Fanny Crosby" because she could sing Fanny Crosby hymns from the very depths of her heart. People often journeyed one hundred miles or more to hear

26

er heart-felt rendition of Fanny's hymn of adoration:

"Praise Him, praise Him, Jesus our blessed Redeemer;
Sing, O earth, His wonderful love proclaim."

On another occasion, a man traveling in the Sahara Desert heard a song drifting toward him from a camp of fierce-looking men. As he recognized the melody from a Fanny Crosby hymn, his fear of spending the night in their camp disappeared. He knew that if they had learned such a hymn, their lives had been influenced by the Bible's message of Jesus Christ. He quickly joined them at the campfire.

Such true accounts of lives enriched by her poems naturally encouraged Fanny's heart. Every year her own Methodist Church held an annual "Fanny Crosby Day" to honor both the poet and her hymns. But her music, leaping the barriers of age, language and religious backgrounds, reached out to all church groups. People of various faiths still enjoy her hymns.

One reason Fanny Crosby's hymns have such wide appeal is that they were written out of the joys and sorrows of everyday living. Fanny knew physical hardship, the joys of love through her marriage to Alexander Van Alstyne, a blind musician. She knew sorrow through the death of her only child in infancy. Through it all, she knew that God makes no mistakes and her poems reflect this quiet faith.

From the age of 80 until her death 14 years later the blind poet lived in Bridgeport, Connecticut, with her widowed sister. On February 12, 1915, after suffering a cerebral hemorrhage, Frances J. Crosby died and met the Lord, who had been her friend for so long. "And I shall see Him face to face," she had prophetically written, "and tell the story saved by grace."

These words are written on her tombstone at the Mount Grove Cemetery. "She hath done what she could." America

27

had become a greater citadel of faith because of her life and hymns and the whole world had caught the refrain of her singing heart!

Harriet Beecher Stowe

Her Book Shook a Nation

CHAPTER FOUR

So this is the little lady who made this big war!" Abraham Lincoln said with a smile as he greeted Harriet Beecher Stowe during the dark days of the Civil War. He was referring, of course, to her controversial anti-slavery novel, *Uncle Tom's Cabin,* a bestseller which helped stir Americans to action about the plight of the slaves. Only a very courageous person could have written such a daring and unusual book. Harriet Beecher Stowe was such a woman.

She was the seventh child and fourth daughter of Lyman Beecher, the famed Congregational minister whose early years of ministry were a perpetual revival. He preached daily and three times on Sunday. Harriet was born on June 14, 1811, in Litchfield, Connecticut. Catharine, her older sister by ten years, became a prominent figure in the education of women during the nineteenth century. Henry Ward, her brother, two years younger than Harriet, influenced thousands by his powerful preaching.

When Harriet was only four, her sensitive and devoutly religious mother, Roxanne, died of "galloping consumption."

Sometime later, her father remarried Harriet Porter, daughter of one of the best known physicians in the Down East county. Harriet, however, could not identify with her new mother, a somber, austere disciplinarian very different from Roxanne. So Harriet turned to her father and Henry for attention and understanding which they freely gave. In Harriet's eyes, her father exemplified "the image of the Heavenly Father," whose powerful leadership made their home "a kind of moral heaven, replete with moral oxygen, fully charged with intellectual electricity." Hungry for knowledge, she spent some of her happiest hours reading good books in her father's library.

At thirteen, Harriet decided to attend The Female Seminary in Hartford, founded by her sisters Catharine and Mary. While there, Harriet penned a blank verse account of the conversion of a young man in Nero's court. During the following summer she had a new experience.

31

But what of Harriet's own soul?

"Harriet's conversion was a simple experience after all. The King of Heaven had spread His table that Sunday and the snowy cloth covering the bread and wine accented her alienage. Only the initiated could partake of the sacred feast. Her father preached from the text, 'I call you not servants but friends.' 'Come, then, and trust your soul to this faithful friend.' Wishfully, she felt a conviction of her sins and tears gathered in her blue eyes as her heart throbbed, 'I will.' That evening she told her father, who pressed her to his breast. She felt tears fall on her head."

"Is it so?" he said. "Then has a new flower blossomed in the Kingdom this day."

"It may not have been the blinding light that struck down Saul of Tarsus, but it would serve one of the most consistently Christ-minded women America ever produced."

This spiritual conversion did not automatically solve all of Harriet's psychological and social problems. She still suffered from the same paralyzing depressions her father often had and felt destined for spinsterhood. Shy, thin, smallboned with the prominent Beecher nose, she considered herself to be "homely and hunch backed" and thought little of herself and her abilities.

Her self image improved, however, when she met Calvin Ellis Stowe, a professor of Biblical Literature at Lane Theological Seminary in Cincinnati. The Beechers had moved there in 1832 when Mr. Beecher accepted the presidency of the school. Stocky, nearsighted, and balding, Calvin was not exactly the dashing hero out of a romantic novel, but he did love Harriet and she in turn loved him. On January 6, 1836, the thirty-three-year-old widower and the twenty-four-year-old president's daughter married.

Their marriage was never smooth. Calvin was given to fits of self-contempt and could become "very comfortably sick" when his moods so dictated. Although a brilliant scholar and teacher, he never discovered how to make enough money to ake care of his wife and their seven children, so Harriet lecided to work.

Always resourceful, Harriet began supplementing her 1usband's income by writing articles and stories. Versatile as he was gifted, she wrote about temperance, New England 1istory, and other popular subjects of her day. In 1843, Harper and Brothers published *The Mayflower,* a collection of 1er stories. Her husband urged her to write her name "fully 1nd always Harriet Beecher Stowe, which is a name euphonious and flowing and full of meaning." Thus her full 1ame appeared on all her writings.

Encouraged by the publication of her first book and weary of the daily pressures from her small children, insufficient ncome, and critical mother-in-law, Harriet told Calvin that she just had to have "a writing room." He agreed, expressing 1imself in his scholarly way. "God has written it in His Book," 1e said, "that you should be a literary woman and who are we hat we should contend against God?"

Simultaneously, both her writing career and personal sorrows gained momentum. Her infant son died in the cholera epidemic of 1849 and her own health broke. She sought treatment far from Brunswick, Maine where her 1usband had settled to teach at Bowdoin College. Finally she vas able to join her husband and renew family living so dear o her heart. Each evening she enthusiastically read Sir Walter Scott's novels to her children for two hours and eventually finished them all.

33

Harriet might have remained merely a reader of stories to her children and a writer of articles and short stories for magazines had not her mind and heart throbbed against slavery, the most serious social cancer of her day. She agonized over such atrocities as slave mothers destroying hemselves after their children were snatched from them and sold; slaves' ears being cut off and their faces and backs oranded and other stories reported by fugitives. These accounts intensified her desire to cry out publicly against "man's inhumanity to man."

Then came the Fugitive Slave Law of 1850 which made it a criminal act to assist runaway slaves. In Brooklyn, her brother Henry denounced this new law from his prestigious pulpit and so did Edward Beecher in Boston. But how could a woman, Harriet wondered, lash out at the pride and prejudice which treated human beings as inanimate objects for sale or trade?

Harriet's answer seemed to be "write a story—a novel, a book to make Americans think and rethink the issue of slavery."

But why, she thought, should *she* as a woman be God's chosen vehicle? Other male contemporaries such as Longfellow, Hawthorne, Emerson, Melville, Thoreau, and Whittier all personally loathed slavery but were already established book authors. Why should she, a housewife-author, dare to attempt what these professionals avoided?

Harriet did not have the answers to these questions, but she *knew* that a story unmasking slavery had to be written. A letter from her sister-in-law, prepared her to take action. "Now Hattie," she wrote, "if I could use a pen as you can, I would write something that would make the whole nation feel what an accursed thing slavery is." After reading these words Harriet Beecher Stowe humbly accepted the assignment to pierce calloused consciences with a story that needed telling.

She conceived the basic plot of *Uncle Tom's Cabin* during a communion service similar to the one when she received Christ as King of her life. This time, however, a vision of the triumphant death of a black man named Tom flashed before her. Who was this man? What joys, what sorrows had he experienced before his release from this life? Using the fundamentals of the Bible story: "a paradise of innocence ... the conflict with principalities, powers, rulers of darkness of this world,—and finally

Paradise regained," she slowly constructed a modern story emphasizing the conflict between good and evil; pulsating with such identifiable emotions as hate, personified by Simon Legree; love, dramatized by Tom and Eva's dying together in anticipation of the New Jerusalem's future glory; faith, expressed by Tom. He was a transparent Christian who, when asked how he knew there is a Christ, answered firmly, "Felt Him in my soul, Mas'r—feel Him now!"

The fast-moving drama of Tom's life first appeared as a serial in National Era, the abolitionist newspaper in 1851, the same year as *Moby Dick* and *The House of Seven Gables* were published. The competition, however, did not diminish the public's appetite for an anti-slavery story. Soon *Uncle Tom's Cabin,* released in book form, was taking America and much of the world by storm.

It sold 300,000 copies in America and one million copies in England in the first twelve months! Eventually the book was translated into 36 languages.

"How she is shaking the world with her *Uncle Tom's Cabin!*" exclaimed Henry Wadsworth Longfellow, the famed poet. "At one step she has reached the top of the staircase up which the rest of us climb on our knees year after year." Even Henry James, a novelist himself, observed that Harriet's novel was 'less a book than a state of vision, of feeling and of consciousness."

Naturally, the popular book triggered controversy. The American South labeled Harriet with abusive terms. Nearly thirty "anti-Uncle Tom" novels burst into print within three years after publication of Harriet's runaway bestseller.

The royalties, however, helped compensate for the adverse criticisms. Harriet and Calvin now could travel extensively. English nobles gave them warm recognition, Scottish crowds cheered them, and the Duchess of Sutherland even gave Harriet a gold bracelet fashioned to look like a slave's shackles.

The Stowes also dined with such illustrious figures as

Thackeray, Dickens, Kingsley, and Gladstone.

For twenty-two years, from 1862 throuth 1884, Harrie produced an average of one book a year. None, however, me with the success of *Uncle Tom's Cabin.* A devoted mother a well as a writer, Harriet once wrote to her publisher's wife "To them (my children) in their needs, I must write chapters which would otherwise go into my novel."

Finally, in her eighty-second year, she confided to Oliver Wendell Holmes, "My brain is tired out ... it gave out before the end was reached." The end came three years later, on July 1, 1896. Doctors diagnosed the cause of death as a brain congestion complicated by partial paralysis.

Harriet Beecher Stowe was laid to rest between her husband and her son, Henry. (Henry accidentally drowned thirty-nine years before.) They are buried in Andover Massachusetts.

Uncle Tom's Cabin, however, lives on and on, reminding each new generation of the Christian faith that shines even in the midnight of man's inhumanity to man.

Emily Dickinson
America's Greatest Woman Poet

CHAPTER FIVE

"**I** have a horror of death," wrote Emily Dickinson. "The dead are so soon forgotten. But when I die, they'll have to remember me."

Her words were prophetic, for today Emily Dickinson *is* remembered. One authority says she is the only nineteenth century woman poet to whom the twentieth century listens.

Because details of her early life offer valuable insights into her literary development and eventually greatness, that is where we must begin.

Emily Elizabeth Dickinson was born December 10, 1830, the second child of Edward and Emily Dickinson. Her religious, austere father kept active in the affairs of Amherst, Massachusetts. He was a lawyer, college official, businessman, politician, a commanding public figure and Puritan churchman who held a firm thumb on his children even after they reached adulthood. For example, Mr. Dickinson, upon learning that his only son, Austin, had plans of practicing law in the Midwest, insisted that he and his wife stay in Amherst and move into the house next door. They did just that! The two Dickinson daughters, Emily and La Vinia, seldom were allowed to wander far from the parental roof.

However, when Emily was fifteen she visited her mother's relatives in Boston and visited all the sights, glorying in the great city. The long stay in the wonderland of Boston over, she returned to Amherst and started college.

Now long country walks, Valentine and sugaring-off maple syrup parties on snow saved until May or June, began for demure, bright, quick Emily who laughingly slashed off comic Valentines, raised flowers and read Shakespeare.

Upon her graduation from Amherst Academy in 1847, Emily went to Mount Holyoke Female Seminary. She did well in her studies but rejected the evangelical fervor of Mary Lyon, founder of the seminary, and her co-workers who held special meetings for non-committed people like Emily whom they felt were "without hope."

Perhaps Emily was rejecting their totalitarian approach and

not their Savior. Whatever her reason, she decided not to return to Holyoke and accepted her father's invitation to return home. She did, however, say just before she left that she would miss the school. "I feel that this world holds a dominant place in my affections," Emily stated, and then took the carriage back home.

Yet she was far from being only an earthling and her poems reveal a soul searching for spiritual reality,

> "Savior! I've no one else to tell
> And so I trouble Thee.
> I am the one forgot Thee so
> Dost Thou remember me?
> Nor, for myself, I came so far
> That were the little load
> I brought Thee the imperial Heart
> I had not strength to hold
> The Heart I carried in my own
> Till mine too heavy grew
> Yet—strangest—heavier since it went
> Is it too large for you?"

Another poem, firmer in its logic and faith, reveals the more peaceful side of Emily's nature:

40

> "I never saw a Moor—
> I never saw the sea—
> Yet know I how the Heather looks
> And what a Billow be.
>
> "I never spoke with God
> Nor visited in Heaven—
> Yet certain am I of the spot
> As if the Checks were given."

Emily began to write poems while in her early twenties.

Perhaps she was inspired by Emerson's poems sent to her by Benjamin F. Newton after he left Amherst. According to Emily, Benjamin had become the "first of my friends" while a law student in her father's office. After Benjamin's death in 1853, she wrote, "My dying Tutor told me that he would like to live till I had been a poet ..."

While visiting Philadelphia, Emily first heard Reverend Charles Wadsworth speaking and his eloquence coupled with a suffering heart appealed to her temperament. She began to write poems for him which he eagerly read. To him she wrote for spiritual advice and treasured a volume of privately printed sermons. Emily wrote 654 poems from 1862 through 1864, continuing to write prolifically even after the death of Reverend Wadsworth, her "closest earthly friend." His passing affected her deeply.

Another cherished friend of Emily's was Thomas Wentworth Higginson, an essayist and critic. He advised her not to publish her poetry with the exception of seven poems which appeared in limited circulation publications. She followed his advice and kept her other 1,768 creations in her bedroom!

Imagine the joys her generation missed by not reading such poems as this:

> "I'm Nobody! Who are you?
> Are you—Nobody—Too?
> Then there's a pair of us?
> Don't tell! they'd advertise—you know!
>
> "How dreary—to be—Somebody!
> How public—like Frog
> To tell one's name—the livelong June
> To an admiring Bog!"

By 1860, Emily had become more than just another witty, well informed young woman. She stripped herself of non-essentials and poetry became her life. Like Thoreau, she found no one "as companionable as solitude." She felt secure in her parents' home or outside in the garden watching the spider "at his trade" and the robin "unroll his feathers." The tall evergreen hedges in the garden formed an effective barricade for Emily against the world.

> "I'll tell you how the Sun rose
> A Ribbon at a time
> The steeples swam in Amethyst
> The news, like Squirrels, ran
> The Hills untied their Bonnets
> The Bobolinks—begun
> Then I said softly to myself
> 'That must have been the Sun'!
> But how he set—I know not
> There seemed a purple stile
> That little Yellow boys and girls
> Were climbing all the while
> Till when they reached the other side,
> A Dominie in Gray
> Put gently up the evening Bars
> And led the flock away."*

42

Behind poetic rhyme and meter Emily also felt safe and painted her word pictures which would later delight the eyes and soul of following generations. There she could express the emotions she so strongly felt. All possibilities such as marriage and even writing for publication involved commitment, a risk she was afraid to take. What masterful strokes she took, nonetheless, when she splashed these phrases on paper.

She could not shield herself, however, from the sorrows

*Poems by Emily Dickinson, copyright 1929, © 1957 by Mary L. Hampson.

within the house. Her father died in 1874 and the following year her mother had a paralytic stroke and died seven years later.

Emily's world brightened for a few years when a widower friend of the family, Judge Otis P. Lord, shared her deep feelings of affection. But they made no wedding plans, evidently knowing that they were too set in their ways for marriage.

In 1884, Judge Lord died of a stroke and Emily's eight-year-old nephew died of typhoid fever. This double loss caused Emily to suffer both a physical and emotional breakdown from which she never fully recovered.

A beautiful Spring day May 15, 1886, Emily Dickinson died at the age of fifty-five from Bright's Disease contracted two-and-a-half years earlier. Austin, who loved her dearly, wrote in his diary, "I was near by." A poem by one of her favorite writers, Emile Bronte, was read. Her white casket covered with violets and ground pine was carried across the field to the family plot by trusted and loved Dickinson servants. Her story and contribution to literature might have ended there had not her practical but unpoetic sister, La Vinia salvaged 1,775 poems Emily had stuffed in her dresser drawers.

Her gravestone reads:

43

Born, Dec. 10, 1830
CALLED BACK
May 15, 1886

Susan B. Anthony

Exponent of Women's Rights

CHAPTER SIX

Susan's warm blue eyes studied the face of her father as he shared with her what he had told the other five children: "Tolerate not evil against humanity. And when thee is powerless to do anything else, speak with vigor. Protest!"

She knew these were more than words to Daniel Anthony. Her memories raced back to the time when as a five-year-old child she accompanied her Quaker father to the home of the local tax collector. Mr. Anthony, proud owner of a successful cotton mill, did not wish to support state policies upholding force of arms. He knew, though, that he had to pay his taxes or suffer the consequences. Finally he decided on a strategy which would be fair to both the government and himself. As Susan watched anxiously, he laid his wallet on the tax collector's table. "I shall not voluntarily pay these taxes," he said firmly, "but if thee wants to steal from my purse, thou can do so." The unsmiling tax collector then reached in, took out the specified amount and handed the wallet back to her father. Susan would never forget this profile in courage.

Born on February 15, 1820, Susan Brownell Anthony grew up in the Quaker community of Adams, Massachusetts. There men and women received fairer treatment than was generally practiced in that day. She soon learned that Quakers could not own slaves and that her people supported the temperance movement. She also discovered the thrill of learning, while attending a rather progressive school where girls could study geography and languages in addition to the three R's and needlework.

In 1858, when Susan was eighteen, she witnessed the most severe economic depression America had ever experienced. After her beloved father declared bankruptcy, creditors seized the mill, their home and even gifts given to Mrs. Anthony by her parents. According to law, anything a married woman had was her husband's and therefore could be seized in payment of his debts.

Susan and her sister Guelma, the two oldest children,

suddenly needed to support themselves. They both found employment as teachers. For the next fifteen years, Susan taught in both private and public schools. The highest wage she ever earned was three dollars a week, minus one dollar for board. Resenting this low estimate of her worth as a teacher, Susan discovered that a male teacher automatically received three times her salary.

Although Susan despised this inequality between men and women, she hesitated to invest her spare time in the new Women's Rights Movement. She chose to fight slavery and liquor instead, becoming the President of the Canajoharie Daughters of Temperance.

When a state convention of the New York State Sons of Temperance was to be held in Syracuse, Susan and Mrs. Amelia Bloomer were appointed to be the delegates. On their arrival, they were informed that the convention had withdrawn the invitation and that they were not welcome to attend the meetings.

Undaunted, Susan and Amelia entered the convention hall. The chairman ordered them to leave. Men jeered at the female duo. One man demanded that no further business be transacted until "these creatures, a hybrid species, half-man and half-woman, belonging to neither sex, are put out." The two women left the room but not in defeat. Susan decided then and there, at age thirty-three, that the Women's Rights Movement was desperately needed. She must help the cause.

At the annual convention of the New York State Teachers Association, Susan seized the opportunity to speak out on behalf of women. Although women made up two-thirds of the membership, the male teachers did all the speaking and the voting. The women came just to listen and observe. Finally, on the second day, Susan could no longer remain silent. Jumping to her feet, she hollered out, "Mr. President." He replied in a disinterested voice, "What will the lady have?" Susan quickly replied, "The lady wishes to speak to the question." As she remained standing, the men debated for hirty minutes whether or not this innovation should be allowed. At last, the men took a vote and a small majority approved her right to express her opinion about why teaching did not command the respect given to other professions.

"It seems to me you fail to comprehend the cause of the disrespect of which you complain," Susan began. "Do you not see that so long as society says woman has not brains enough to be a doctor, lawyer or minister, but has plenty to be a teacher, every man of you, who condescends to teach, tacitly admits before all Israel and the sun that he has no more brains than a woman?" She then sat down, having made her point, the meeting immediately broke up. Some women teachers congratulated her on her courage as they walked out; others drew in their skirts as they passed her at the door.

Next morning, a Mrs. Northrop asked for the floor and read a resolution that the New York Teachers Association recognize "the rights of female teachers to share in all the privileges and deliberations of this body." The resolution carried. Written by Mrs. Northrop and Susan B. Anthony, it marked Susan's first victory in her battle against male dominance.

Later Susan shared her conviction that this movement needed a permanent functioning with Elizabeth Cady Standon, one of the leaders of the Woman's Rights Movement. Believing an immediate goal of an organization supported by thousands would marshall everyone into action, Susan laid plans for a convention to be held in Rochester, New York. She drew up a Declaration of Rights, which stated among other matters that married women have a right to the money they earn and the children to whom they gave birth. Trudging from house to house, Susan and her appointed aides secured the signatures of ten thousand women!

Although the convention attracted a large attendance, the Legislature in Albany ridiculed the petitions written by Susan B. Anthony and her followers. Both bills presented by the convention were rejected by the legislature.

"We will be back," Susan told the legislators. "We will be back again and again until laws are enacted to give women their due rights." Realizing her need of more public support, she planned to lecture in as many New York counties as possible. With fifty dollars, a carpetbag filled with petitions and a heart full of faith and courage, she left Rochester by train on Christmas Day, 1854. In some towns she had good turnouts and generous responses to her appeal for funds. Other places refused to let her use a church or schoolhouse to discuss the "detestable woman's doctrine."

To advance her cause she willingly endured physical discomforts. When snowstorms prevented her from reaching her destination in time to eat, she went hungry. Her body became frost bitten during the coldest winter New York had known in ten years. Her back began aching from constant travel over rough roads and sleeping on uncomfortable beds in cold village inns.

Sore but joyous, Susan returned to Rochester on the first of May. From her lectures in fifty-four out of sixty counties, she had obtained many signatures and $2,367! Armed with these additional names and public support, she again journeyed to Albany and presented the cause of women's rights. Again, she was turned down. This action was repeated six different times. Finally, with patience running thin, Susan and her supporters tried once more. This time, their seventh appearance before the New York Legislature turned the tide. In March, 1860, Legislature adopted a bill which granted married women rights to their own property and earnings, to sue and be sued, to enter into contracts and to be equal guardians of their children. Susan had fulfilled her vow to the legislators to "be back again and again until the laws are enacted giving women their due rights."

As her fame spread, invitations to speak poured in from distant states. For some time she traveled in the Mid and Farwestern states lecturing on behalf of the Anti-Slavery

Society. Many towns had never seen or heard a woman lecturer. Curious people often came in wagonloads to see the valiant woman who hated injustice of any kind and was not afraid to say so.

Blessed with a quick wit, she had a ready reply for any critic. On one occasion, an abolitionist speaker named Reverend A. D. Mayo told Susan that she had no business discussing marriage because she was single. She replied that since he was not a slave he should quit lecturing on slavery.

During the Kansas campaign for women's suffrage, the famed anti-slavery publisher Horace Greeley asked, "Miss Anthony, you know the ballot and the bullet go together. If you vote, are you ready to fight?" She replied, "Yes, Mr. Greeley, just as you fought in the Civil War, at the point of a goose quill."

Susan shared the belief of many women that the Fourteenth Amendment, which gave the Negro the right to vote, also entitled a woman to the same privilege. Congress had defined a citizen as any person born or naturalized in the United States and had made no mention of sex. On November 1, 1872, Susan decided to test the validity of the Fourteenth Amendment. Heading up a group of fifteen brave women, she led them to the polling headquarters for Rochester's eighth ward. There she told unnerved election inspectors that her group had come to enroll as voters. Told that such enrollment would be illegal, the reformer pulled out a copy of the United States Constitution and said, "Prove it!"

Grudgingly, the men enrolled all sixteen women, three of whom were Susan's married sisters. On election day, when they cast their votes, newspapers splashed the incident across their front pages. Editorials labeled Susan B. Anthony and her friends willful lawbreakers. Editors argued that if these women were not punished, every woman in the United States would think herself enfranchised. The administration of

49

President Ulysses S. Grant agreed and made plans to prosecute the Rochester women.

When Susan answered the door on Thanksgiving Day, a United States marshall produced a warrant for her arrest. "You may go to the courthouse without me," he said apologetically. "Oh dear, no," the spunky fifty-two-year-old countered. "I much prefer to be taken, handcuffed if possible." He refused to put her in handcuffs but he did escort her to the courthouse where the fifteen women voters and an attorney stood waiting. The lawyer, Henry B. Selden, had been hired by Susan in case of trouble.

The women all pleaded not guilty to a charge of voting illegally in a national election. The judge then set bail at $500. Each of the fifteen put up bail money but Susan refused, demanding her release on a writ of habeas corpus. The judge denied her request and increased her bail to $1,000. Once more, she refused bail and wondered why she was not taken to jail. Later she learned that Selden had put up bail without her knowledge. "I could not see a lady go to jail," he explained to his client.

After learning that her group would not be tried until the summer of 1873, Susan felt responsible for instigating the controversial incident. She decided to go on a lecture tour to earn enough to pay the trial costs.

Titling her lecture, "Is It A Crime for a United States Citizen to Vote?" she successfully toured the Midwest. Everywhere large and receptive audiences greeted her.

Exhausted from her travel and speaking engagements, she returned home to rest. She would need all the strength she could muster to cope with the pressures of the forthcoming trial. Unknown to her during this time, the government had its own ideas as to how the trial should go and what the verdict should be. In charge of the strategy was United States Senator Roscoe Conkling, the Republican boss of New York State. He decided to try Susan B. Anthony, the "Woman Napoleon" instead of the sixteen women. It would be easier, he reasoned, to convict one controversial woman than some unknown housewives.

On a bright June day, Susan B. Anthony's trial began in the Canandaigua courthouse. On the bench was none other than a Justice of the Supreme Court, the Honorable Ward Hunt. Newsmen made note of an Associate Justice of the U.S. Supreme Court being assigned to try a case in the Circuit Court.

The dramatic trial lasted only two days. After the prosecuting attorney had stated the case against Susan, Selden, her attorney, asked that his client be granted the privilege of testifying in her own defense. Judge Hunt denied the motion, because the client was a woman and therefore not competent to testify.

The "fixed" trial proceeded, with Judge Hunt stating that he would act for the defendant by reading the testimony she had given at her hearing. After he had finished reading, the prosecutor made a brief summation and Selden presented his passionate defense arguments.

Then Judge Hunt turned to the jury, proclaiming the fact that Susan had voted illegally and therefore was not protected by the Constitution. He charged the jury that "The result must be a verdict on your part of guilty, and I therefore direct that you find a verdict of guilty."

Selden protested but was ignored. Judge Hunt then told the clerk of the court to "take the verdict." The clerk mumbled, "Gentlemen of the jury, hearken to your verdict as the court has recorded it. You say you find the defendant guilty of the offense whereof she stands indicted, and so say you all," and then sat down.

The jury had not said a word! The trial and the script had been prepared by the political machinery determined to find Susan guilty!

The next day she appeared at court to receive her sentence. Selden frowned, expecting a fine of $500 and a three-year prison sentence also.

51

Confident of his success, Judge Hunt asked, "Has the prisoner anything to say why sentence should not be pronounced?"

"Yes, Your Honor, I have many things to say," Susan answered confidently, "for in your ordered verdict of guilty you have trampled underfoot every vital principle of our government. My natural rights, my civil rights, my political rights are all ignored. Robbed of the fundamental privilege of citizenship, I am degraded from the status of citizen to that of subject; and not only myself individually but all of my sex are by Your Honor's verdict doomed to political subjection."

Noticing newsmen jotting down every word, the judge realized that the free publicity for the Women's Rights Movement had to be stopped. "The court cannot listen to a—" he began to say, but her clear voice drowned him out. "... All my prosecutors," she continued, "from the eighth ward corner grocer politician who entered the complaint, to the United States marshall, commissioner, district attorney, district judge, Your Honor on the bench, not one is my peer, but each and all my political sovereigns. And had Your Honor submitted my case to the jury, as was clearly your duty, even then I should have had just cause for protest, for none of these men was my peer; but native or foreign, white or black, rich or poor, educated or ignorant, awake or asleep, sober or drunk, each and every man of them was my political superior."

Red-faced, Judge Hunt shouted, "The prisoner will sit down!"

But Susan would not sit down or be quiet. Her feelings from twenty years of reform work flowed out like lava from an erupting volcano. Finally, the judge rapped for order. "The prisoner has been tried according to established forms of law," he announced.

Susan retorted, "Yes, Your Honor, but by forms of law made by men, interpreted by men, administered by men, in favor of men—and against women." She continued talking and concluded with these words, "I ask not leniency at your hands, but to take the full rigors of law."

Glaring with indignation, Judge Hall pronounced sentence, assigning Susan a fine of $100 plus court costs.

"I shall never pay a dollar of your unjust penalty," she declared. And she kept her word. She paid no fine and she stayed out of jail. Both the judge and Susan knew that if she had been sent to jail, the case would have gone to the Supreme Court on a writ of habeas corpus.

Subsequent newspaper coverage of the "fixed" trial triggered sympathy and support for the cause of Women's rights. Susan B. Anthony became a symbol of personal progress in America. As President of the National Woman Suffrage Association, she helped prepare the way for the Nineteenth Amendment that gave the right to vote to women. Unfortunately, it was not passed until 1920, fourteen years after her death.

Susan *knew* success was just around the corner. In March of 1906, at a women's rights meeting in Washington, celebrating her 86 birthday, she gave a brief talk to her supporters. Her speech ended with three memorable words: "Failure is impossible."

A few days later, Susan B. Anthony died from pneumonia. She had lived life fully and had obeyed her father's command to never "tolerate evil against humanity" but to "speak with vigor." Daniel Anthony could be justly proud of his blue-eyed daughter!

Helen Keller

Conqueror of a Double Handicap

CHAPTER SEVEN

Frustration and hopelessness gripped the hearts of Arthur and Kate Keller. How much longer could they endure the ordeal of watching their six-year-old daughter grope her way around the sunny rooms and wide halls of their beautiful Southern home?

Four long years had dragged by since nineteen-month-old Helen had suffered the prolonged illness which robbed her of both sight and hearing. They had taken her to doctor after doctor but the opinions were unanimous: "Your daughter will never see or hear again."

Locked in her dark and silent prison, Helen's emotions raged, demanding expression. But all she could do, with no words to convey her feelings, was to throw herself on the floor in fits of rage or weep bitterly.

Then, one day in her sixth year, Helen's parents were advised by an old and kindly doctor to take her to Alexander Graham Bell, whose concern for the deaf had caused him to find a way to send sound over wire.

The great inventor listened to the concerned parents and then recommended that they contact the Perkins Institution for the Blind in Boston. He told them that years ago, a deaf and blind girl, Laura Bridgman, had been successfully educated at Perkins.

Overjoyed, Captain and Mrs. Keller asked Perkins to send them a teacher for Helen. On March 3, 1887, Anne Sullivan arrived.

Miss Sullivan placed a rag doll in Helen's arms, a doll which Laura, the educated deaf and blind girl, had dressed. Then she reached for Helen's arm and slowly wrote in her palm the word "D-O-L-L." Miss Sullivan repeated this again and again, hoping that Helen would associate these markings with the doll gripped tightly in her skinny arms. But the realization would not come and Helen remained in fear of her surroundings.

A month later, however, Helen finally understood what all the hand-writing was about. While she and Miss Sullivan were walking together down a winding path, Miss Sullivan's arm suddenly moved up and down and then something cold hit Helen's hand. "W-A-T-E-R," spelled the teacher into her student's hand, "W-A-T-E-R" ... "W-A-T-E-R." The law of association burst into Helen's mind, driving out the darkness of the unknown. Now she knew that everything had a name! "W-A-T-E-R" was the name of that cold liquid! "D-O-L-L" was the name of that warm thing she held in her arms! Eagerly she touched the hard thing from which the water flowed. "P-U-M-P," wrote Miss Sullivan.

She next touched that something under her feet. "G-R-O-U-N-D" wrote the patient lady who had opened this new world to her.

"Who was this new person in her life?" Helen asked through hand motions.

"T-E-A-C-H-E-R," came the reply.

Hand in hand with her teacher, Helen dashed around the yard touching, asking, learning. In a few hours she had learned thirty new names!

Using techniques she gradually learned, within six months Helen could spell and make sentences from 600 words. She used signals and gestures for words "hat" and "walk" which meant, "Get your hat and we will go for a walk."

Obviously, without sight or hearing, she still had difficulty understanding many things. For example, she had felt the vibrations as baby chicks pecked their way through eggshells. Therefore, when she felt the squirming body of a little pig, she naturally asked, "Did baby pig grow in a shell?"

In spite of such wrong guesses, she remained such an undaunted student that Miss Sullivan told Helen's parents she was ready to begin studying in a classroom situation with other children. They agreed and within a few weeks Helen and Miss Sullivan were in Boston, walking toward the famed Perkins Institution for the Blind.

It wasn't long before Helen was conversing with other blind students at school, using the language of the hand. She also began to read books printed in raised type after Miss Sullivan taught her the shape of each letter using slips of cardboard.

Deciding on a novel way to give Helen her first history lesson, Miss Sullivan took her to historic Bunker Hill and had her count each step as the climbed the monument. After that trip, they went by steamboat to Plymouth and studied about the Pilgrims. Fascinated by the ocean, Helen asked, "Who put salt in the water?"

Helen's life at Perkins was basically smooth and enjoyable until she made the discovery by feeling the movement of people's lips and the vibration of their throats, that many people were deaf but still could speak.

Determined, Helen told Miss Sullivan that she "wanted to be able to talk as the other people did."

Obligingly, Miss Sullivan took her to an expert in the field of speech. Early in 1890 when Helen was still at Perkins, the first lesson began. She learned the six elements of speech—M,P,A,S,T,I. Ten more lessons then followed, by far the most difficut lessons the ten-year-old student had ever attempted. She could not hear her own voice and consequently her words were indistinct. She became discouraged but refused to quit. By the end of her eleventh lesson she talked endlessly to everybody and every-thing—dolls, books, even the birds. Her words gradually became understandable to others beside her teachers.

Her personal mission accomplished, she notified Miss Sullivan that now she had to speak to three very special people—her parents and younger sister.

The two companions bought train tickets in November, 1890 for Tuscumbia, Alabama, Helen's hometown. To the ten-year-old, tingling with excitement, the train seemed to barely crawl its way from the East Coast to the Deep South. But finally they arrived and the three Kellers met them anxiously at the train station. As they came face to face, Helen slowly and clearly said the first sentence she had learned to speak: "I am not dumb now!"

Imagine the tidal wave of emotions caused by those five short words! Helen later wrote, "my mother pressed me close, speechless and trembling." What stories the walls of the Keller home could tell if they could repeat the love and merriment of that enchanted evening when Helen's voice joined her family's at home! She expressed her recollection in the words of Isaiah 55:12, "The mountains and the hills shall break forth before you into singing."

Even this herculean accomplishment, however, did not satisfy Helen's heart. She desired to create, to put words on paper which would express the deep feelings in her soul. At twelve she wrote a short story of her life which *Youth's Companion* accepted and published. Her writing career had begun.

In 1902, 22 years of age, Helen began a book titled *The Story of My Life* in monthly installments contracted by The Ladies Home Journal for $3,000. Helen was enchanted but soon was frightened out of her wits as telegrams came thick and fast, "We must have the next chapter immediately."

During this prolific period, Helen began helping her fellow-sufferers, the blind and the handicapped of the world. While still a pre-teen her first venture raised two thousand dollars for a kindergarten for blind children.

At the age of thirteen, Helen decided to visit the current World's Fair held at Niagara Falls. Because of her handicap, she was granted special permission to touch the exhibits so that she could "see them with her fingers." Miss Sullivan and Alexander Graham Bell watched her face radiate happiness as she examined the telephone, the phonograph and other discoveries. Both felt that perhaps no one enjoyed the Fair as much as the teen-age blind and deaf girl.

Helen applied the same zest for life in her studies. After her years at Perkins, Helen decided to prepare herself for college. She entered the Cambridge School for young women determined to take all the regular courses required of the other students. Miss Sullivan went along, spelling the instructors' words into Helen's hand.

Successfully completing the work at Cambridge, Helen chose Radcliffe College as her next world to conquer. When Braille textbooks were not available, Miss Sullivan used the old handwriting method of communication to share the necessary data with her student. Helen used a typewriter to prepare the written assignments.

Her years at Radcliffe were not easy ones, for such advanced learning is difficult even with perfect eyesight and hearing. Helen, however, persisted and graduated from Radcliffe in 1904, completing the required course in four years—the same length of time given students without physical handicaps.

Helen now felt on top of her problems. She knew French, Latin and German and had studied arithmetic, physical geography, lip reading and voice culture and a host of other subjects. Finally prepared to devote her talents, time and energies to helping other blind people, she longed to take them out of their drab world of continual night and show them the road to productivity and light. Because of this magnificent obsession, Helen Keller served on the Massachusetts Commission for the Blind and other agencies designed to help the handicapped help themselves.

She lived a courageous long and fruitful life from June 27, 1880 to June 1, 1968, demonstrating that success comes not from the absence of difficulties but rather from the mastery of attitudes and circumstances.

Clara Barton
The Angel of the Battlefield
CHAPTER EIGHT

Clara probably never heard about the concept of "active retirement," but if anyone was "active" at seventy-seven, it was this dynamic five-foot Good Samaritan. The roar of the cannon during the Spanish-American War meant only one thing to Clara. It was another opportunity to serve the sick and the dying. Bumping along by mule wagon under the burning sun, she served soup to the soldiers and established homes of care for innocent Cuban children suffering in an adult world. Before the War ended, Clara supervised the distribution of 6,000 tons of provisions, valued at half a million dollars.

Such service, typical of her humanitarian spirit, drew Clara out of her shell of shyness and loneliness. "In the early years of my life, I remember nothing but fear," she once wrote. But the change from cowardice to courage did not come easily.

Born Christmas Day, 1821, in North Oxford, Massachusetts, Clara was the fifth and last child of Stephen and Sarah Barton. Soon her practical, warm-hearted mother taught Clara how to excel at household tasks. Her father, on the other hand, instilled into her heart the love of country, concern for people and a special interest in the military. A veteran of the Revolutionary War, he delighted his daughter with wartime adventures, especially tales of their daring leader, "Mad" Anthony Wayne.

"But what happened to the soldiers who got shot?" Clara would ask.

"Well," Mr. Barton would answer, "I really can't tell you because we had to leave them behind so we could chase the Redcoats away..."

She always nodded at her father's explanation but in her mind she pictured poor soldiers dying without water for their parched lips, lacking words of comfort in their final hour. She knew that someday, if she had the opportunity, she would like to help relieve the suffering of these men in uniform.

Her opportunity came when she was only eleven years old. Her brother David injured himself in a fall from a high building. Month after month he battled to get better; and his sister lovingly stayed at his side, fluffing his pillows, entertaining him with stories, news happenings and giving him sparkling well water to quench his feverish thirst.

Two long years passed before David could return to work. By this time his sister was thirteen, well experienced in cheering and helping a victim of pain. Later she would draw on this valuable experience in her service to others.

At this time, however, Clara planned to be a school teacher. She attended both the summer and winter terms at the country schoolhouse two miles up the road from the Barton home. Not content to take only the prescribed subjects, she would seek out teachers to help her study such advanced subjects as chemistry, philosophy and Latin.

At the age of eighteen, with a well-developed mind and increased self-confidence, she determined to find a school board who would hire her. Knowing that they would likely question her youthfulness, she made herself look as mature and as qualified as possible by lengthening her dresses and winding her hair in fashionable coils about her head.

Her plan succeeded and she began teaching in neighboring schools. She quickly became a favorite with her students, who liked her sense of humor, patience and ability to inspire.

Naturally, the popular schoolteacher with wavy brown hair attracted the single men of the area. Although she liked men and they liked her, she turned down three marriage proposals, choosing instead the company of both male and female friends who shared her ideals and values.

Clara taught school for twenty-five years. In 1852, she persuaded the school board of Bordentown, New Jersey, to let her establish one of the first "free" or public schools in that state. The school succeeded so well that by 1854, the board appointed a man over her. Perplexed, Clara resigned and moved to Washington, D.C., where she secured a clerkship in the Patent Office. It is believed that she may have been the first regularly appointed woman civil servant in the history of the U.S.A.

Her work at the Patent Office was as successful as her teaching had been. As the only woman clerk, she sought to find the causes of the department's chronic problems. She trailed some of the tangles back to mistakes made in the past by male clerks. Some of these men were dismissed. Authorities then asked her to continue her work. The Democratic victory of 1857, however, deprived Clara of her position and she returned to North Oxford. Nothing of significance happened during the next three years. Finally, in late 1860, the Patent Office called her back to work.

As the dark clouds of internal strife appeared on the horizon, signaling the beginning of the Civil War, Clara found herself caught up in the conflict that raged around Washington, D.C.. She began her work by offering aid and friendship to homesick Massachusetts soldiers. Then, shocked at the meager first aid facilities at the battle of Bull Run, Clara bought an advertisement in a New England newspaper which appealed for bandages, medicines, foods and provisions for the wounded. The public responded generously. Clara and a few friends traveled by muleteam all over Virginia and Maryland distributing supplies to camps, hospitals and often battlefields. "If heaven ever sent out a holy angel, she must be one," wrote an observer. "Her assistance was so timely."

On one occasion, Clara found an army surgeon trying to care for a thousand suffering men by the light of one lone two-inch candle. Quickly she took out, not one, but four boxes of candles, which enabled the surgeon to help more of the men. Soldiers remembered her as "The Angel of the Battlefield."

Besides her efficient and sympathetic outlook, she also had a spirit of resourcefulness which marveled all who watched her in action. She seemed to never be at a loss. For example, one day when no food supplies had been received, Clara discovered the medicine bottles were packed in fine meal. Going to a nearby farmhouse, she borrowed several big kettles and cooked a meal to serve her famished patients.

Through all these experiences, she remained optimistic and fearless. In a letter to those back home, she wrote: "I wrung the blood from the bottom of my clothing before I could step, for the weight about my feet ..."

She served on sixteen battlefields during the Civil War and never received one injury, although often shell-fire tore her clothing. On one occasion Clara stooped to lift the head of a wounded soldier and a bullet passed between her arm and her body, killing the man she had stopped to help. Another time, as Clara and an escort crossed a pontoon bridge at Fredericksburg under heavy fire, a bullet screamed by and killed her escort. Clara continued her journey alone, knowing that thousands of wounded people needed the help she had to give.

Perhaps her fearless dedication stemmed from her memory of the conversation she had with her father when he lay on his deathbed. He told her to "follow the cannon," because the lack of medical care on the battlefield itself was the greatest cause of death in any war. Thus the battlefield became his daughter's place of service. Writing to a friend, Clara said, "If you chance to feel that the positions I occupied were rough and unseemly for a woman, I can only reply that they were rough and unseemly for a man." Later, she observed, "Everybody's business is nobody's business ... nobody's business is my business."

After the Civil War ended, Clara still "followed the cannon," as it were, by devoting several years to tracing missing soldiers. "Where is my son buried?" a mother would write. Clara would then list the name along with thousands of others and mail the lists to newspapers to publish in their column. As information poured in from soldiers and others who had known these missing men, Clara and her co-workers classified and forwarded the details to concerned families.

64

In February, 1865, President Lincoln gave official approval to Clara Barton's office at Annapolis. In July of that same year, Clara, assisted by a man who had been in charge of the "death roll" while a prisoner at Andersonville, directed the marking of the graves of the nearly 13,000 men who had suffered and died in that terrible Georgia prison.

The following year, Congress reimbursed Clara $15,000 for the heavy expenses involved in such a herculean undertaking. Then, from 1866 to 1868, "The Angel of the Battlefield" traveled extensively throughout the Northern and Western States, speaking on 300 lecture platforms of her memorable Civil War experiences. An effective speaker, she was widely acclaimed as a "war heroine."

In late 1868, exhausted and voiceless, Clara went to her doctor. He urged her to take a lengthy time of recuperation in Europe. Little did either the doctor or Clara imagine that during this time of relaxation she would discover a concept so vital that the rest of her life would be devoted to its fulfillment.

While in Switzerland, Clara heard more and more about the International Committee of the Red Cross formed in Geneva in 1863. Its founder, Jean Henri Dunant, had been so disturbed by the suffering at the battlefield of Solferino in 1859 that he had determined to take steps to diminish the misery of the fighting men. Eleven governments had agreed to the newly written Geneva Treaty, which neutralized the wounded of any country under the red cross on a white background.

Strengthened in body and quickened in spirit, Clara returned to America and began a five-year campaign for the organization of the American Red Cross Society. However, America did not wish to adhere to the Geneva Treaty. Americans felt that with the war days over, it was not necessary to support an organization that gave assistance to soldiers.

Through hard work and persuasion, Clara eventually

convinced her people that the Red Cross could function in peacetime, by providing organized relief for such domestic disasters as floods, droughts, fires, railway accidents and yellow fever scourges.

Convinced by her arguments and pleasant manner, President Garfield promised Clara that America would affiliate with the International Red Cross but was assassinated before he could fulfill his promise. Some time passed before the next chief executive, President Arthur, signed the Geneva Treaty.

While the political wheels ground very slowly, Clara and her friends advanced steadily, organizing the American Association of the Red Cross in May, 1881. The Association then chose Clara Barton to be its first president.

In 1900, Clara and her friends finally received what they had been working so hard to obtain, a federal charter from the Congress of the United States. The American Red Cross had gone through nineteen years of effort, opposition and adverse criticism to reach this milestone.

During the twenty-three years Clara served as its president, the American Red Cross gained a reputation for frugality and efficiency. Clara and her team accomplished their mammoth relief missions with only two million dollars, a small sum when spread over more than twenty years!

66

Clara also emphasized the need for rehabilitation, arguing that giving people relief was not enough. People also needed help to resume their livelihoods. For example, after the devastating hurricane in 1900 that hit Galveston, Texas, the American Red Cross provided one-and-a-half million strawberry plants to help destitute farmers resume their industry.

In spite of all her good accomplishments, Clara Barton became the object of more and more criticism, especially from people within her own organization. As she grew older, she had difficulty delegating authority and adapting newer business procedures.

In 1904, Clara resigned from the presidency of the organization she had founded after twenty-three years of service. Eight years later, in 1912, she died at the age of ninety-one and was buried in her hometown of North Oxford, Massachusetts.

Clara Barton had known perhaps more than her share of life and death, success and failure, praise and criticism. After the Johnstown, Pennsylvania Flood, where the American Red Cross served so faithfully, Clara said, "The paths of charity are over roadways of ashes, and he who would tread them must be prepared to meet opposition, misconstruction, jealousy and calumny. Let his work be that of angels, still it will not satisfy all."

Pocahontas

Indian Heroine of Early America

CHAPTER NINE

W hen Powhatan, the great chief of
'idewater, Virginia, started calling his daughter
Pocahontas" instead of her given name "Matoaka," he had
no idea that her nickname, meaning "frolicsome," would live
on for hundreds of years, reminding history students of the
most colorful Indian heroine to cross the American scene.

Pocahontas, born around 1595 in Virginia, is best
remembered for saving the life of Captain John Smith when
only thirteen years old. Captain Smith, an explorer and
prominent settler of Jamestown, records the event in his
journal using the language of his day: "... Taken prisoner by
the power of Powhatan their chiefe King," he writes, "I
receiused from this great Saluage exceeding great courtesie,
especially from his sonne Nantaquaus ... and his sister,
Pocahontas, the King's most deare and wel-beloued daughter,
being but a childe of twelue or thirteen yeeres of age, whose
compassionate pitifull heart, of my desperate estate, gaue me
much cause to respect her: I being the first Christian this
proud King and his grim attendants euer saw: ... After some
six weeks fatting amongst these Saluage Courtiers, at the
minute of my execution, she (Pocahontas) hazarded the
beating out of her own braines to saue mine, and not onely
that, but so preuailed with her father, that I was safely
conducted to Jamestowne ..."

This account, written nearly ten years after his deliverance
from the Indians in 1607, is the basis for the true story of
Pocahontas. Like most historical accounts, it has been
amplified and made more colorful to the point of becoming a
legend. The facts remain, however, that Pocahontas was a
real person who did indeed save the life of Captain Smith.
The following year, in 1608, Powhatan's Indians made food
available to the Colonists and Pocahontas herself often
brought needed supplies. From that point on, the Indian
princess played a vital role in the relationships between the
whites and her people. She even secured the release of Indian
prisoners.

In 1612, Pocahontas was captured, kept as a princess, a willing prisoner, and taken by boat down the Potomac to Virginia. While there, she learned the English language and the Christian religion. The Reverend Alexander White, missionary and minister, who became her tutor in spiritual matters, patiently instructed her in the teachings of the Bible. After becoming a Christian, she was baptized and chose the Christian name "Rebecca." After her capture a message was sent to Powhatan to release Englishmen detained in slavery, stolen arms, tools and corn.

Pocahontas met John Rolfe, a colonist and a widower ten years her senior. She married him the following year and Chief Powhatan gave the newly weds a tract of land for their wedding present. But history does not record whether they ever lived on it, nor does it reveal the birthplace of their only child, Thomas. Pocahontas' marriage brought peace with the Indians.

Evidence indicates that Sir Thomas Dale, Marshall of Virginia, invited the Rolfe family to sail with him for England. After their arrival in June, 1616, most of the London society warmly received the "Indian Princess" who could converse in English and had adapted herself to the white man's culture.

As a final honor, Pocahontas was invited to the court of King James I and Queen Anne. On January 6, 1617, the royal couple and their American friends went to see *The Vision of Delight* by the famed Ben Jonson. Uttamatomakkin, her father's councillor, accompanied Pocahontas dressed in native garb.

It is difficult to know what Pocahontas thought of the exciting days of sightseeing and accomplishments, but the Indian Princess did want to stay in England longer. Her husband, however, insisted in March that it was time to return to Virginia and get back to work. So, heavyhearted, Pocahontas boarded the ship for America. Contrary winds arose, delaying the ship's departure. The twenty-two-year-old

Princess died before the vessel could leave the Thames River or the open sea. One historian's account says she was a victim of the wet and blustery winter, while another indicates she died of smallpox. She was buried on March 21, 1617, at Gravesend, England.

The story of Pocahontas disappeared for nearly a century until, little by little, writers in the 1700's began to mention the Indian Princess and her heroism. Finally, she became the subject of at least two dramatic productions, *Pocahontas: The Gentle Savage* and a production by George Custis, presented in Philadelphia, 1830. Twentieth century poets such as Carl Sandburg, Vachel Lindsay and others continued to remember the young girl whose life symbolizes the courage that helped make America great.

A bronze statue in Indian dress by John Brougham in New York, stands to her memory in Jamestown, Virginia. The painting, "Baptism of Pocahontas" is exhibited in the rotunda of the United States Capitol.

Elizabeth Blackwell

America's First Woman Doctor

CHAPTER TEN

Small and shy, Elizabeth didn't look like a woman who would challenge the structure of America's medical profession. However, inside her heart pulsated the conviction that women should have the right to care for other women. When a friend dying of cancer told Elizabeth that her worst torment was having to go to a male doctor for help, Elizabeth became more determined than ever to be America's first woman medical school graduate.

She knew the road ahead would not be an easy one. Her determination to become a doctor would be radically different from the general male viewpoint and most of the female outlook as well. Medical science was for men only, people felt, and obstetrics was for midwives.

Born in Bristol, England, in 1821, Elizabeth came with her family to America at age eleven and settled in Cincinnati. After her father died, Elizabeth and her sisters ran a boarding school to support their younger brothers still at home. Finally, when her brothers could fend for themselves, Elizabeth traveled to Philadelphia to enroll in a medical school and was refused. The same rejection was repeated in New York.

"Go to Paris," a friend advised. "Remember the story of the Frenchwoman who took a medical course disguised as a man." Elizabeth smiled. She might have to go to Europe someday. But first, she would contact all the small Eastern institutions. Her inquiries brought twelve more letters of rejection before she received an affirmative reply from the medical school at Geneva, New York.

When she arrived at Geneva two weeks later, she discovered that her acceptance there had resulted from the faculty jokingly asking the students how they would like to have a would-be woman doctor on campus! The Geneva male students thinking this would be fun, voted to accept the woman with "the impossible dream."

Her presence, however, created problems. The male professor of anatomy suggested that Elizabeth did not need the course he taught. She replied in writing, "I need to study as much as any student in the world." Finally the professor gave his consent for her to attend his classes.

Elizabeth also faced rejection off-campus. The townspeople stared at her as if she were some kind of curiosity. "She's the only woman student among five hundred men," the gossips snickered. No local resident wanted to rent a room to her.

Little by little, however, her dedication and determination gained her the respect of the faculty and their wives. Those who had refused to rent to her now tried to be kind to her, ashamed of their attitudes.

Finally, in 1849, after two years of intensive study, Elizabeth Blackwell graduated from the Geneva Medical School at the head of her class! But once again, she faced a closed door. American hospitals refused to give her an internship. So she sailed to Paris and enrolled in the midwives' training school. Before she enrolled, however, she had such memorable experiences as being smuggled into a morgue to operate on a corpse!

After her French schooling, Elizabeth returned to the United States and settled in New York City. Immediately, opposition began as medical men feared they would lose many of their women patients to her. Such was not the case, however. New York women refused to trust a woman doctor!

So, to bridge the credibility gap, Dr. Blackwell started giving lectures on health to women. Many of them, after hearing her medical knowledge and seeing her compassion for people, decided they would dare to receive treatment at her hands!

She next opened an infirmary where people unable to pay standard medical fees could come and be treated without charge. There Elizabeth and her younger sister, Dr. Emily Blackwell, taught poverty-stricken mothers how to practice personal hygiene and care for their children. The infirmary also gave women doctors a place in which to serve their internships. Dr. Blackwell is credited with founding

America's first school of nursing in 1857.

Philadelphia, where Elizabeth had been refused training, finally chartered the first Female Medical School. Other schools followed until by the time of the Civil War three hundred women doctors and surgeons were serving the Union Armies.

Dr. Blackwell lived until 1910, long enough to see women firmly established in the medical profession. Her "impossible dream" had come true. In anticipation of change, she had once written, "The new hope for the world that I see dawning with the advent of womanhood into the realm of independent thought and equal justice makes me very happy."

Frances Willard

Crusader for Temperance

CHAPTER ELEVEN

When their father asked them to "sign the hand-written pledge in the family Bible," the three Willard children showed no hesitation. They had seen the shocking way liquor had turned a man they knew into a virtual beast.

These four lines expressed their feelings against intemperance and their desire to live the Christian life without the shackles of an enslaving habit.

> "To quench our thirst we'll always bring
> Cold Water from the well or spring.
> So here we pledge perpetual hate
> To all that can intoxicate."

Solemnly, they signed their names under "the pledge," Oliver, Frances and Mary. A sincere act typical of the family's decisiveness. As Frances later recalled, "The name Willard, you know, means he who wills."

Born September 28, 1839, in Churchville, New York, Frances soon earned the reputation of being a redheaded tomboy. Preferring to be called "Frank" rather than "Frances," she delighted in jumping fences, climbing trees and riding horseback. She was an adventurous pioneer at heart, just like her parents who had moved from New York state to Ohio and then on to Rock River near Janesville, Wisconsin.

As years passed, Frances outgrew the tomboy stage and became a lovely young lady. "Next to being an angel," she said, "the greatest bestowment of God is to make one a woman."

Determined to be the woman God wanted her to be, she decided to excel in the field of education and enrolled at the Milwaukee Female College. Later, she transferred to the Northwestern Female College at Evanston, Illinois, from which she graduated.

Frances became a good teacher and years later accepted the

presidency of the Evanston (Illinois) College for Women. Although successful and secure, her heart became more and more restless. Her personality demanded more than a job. She desired a cause big enough to live for and to die for and she found it in the Woman's Christian Temperance Union. Already this movement, proving its effectiveness, had closed two hundred and fifty saloons in Ohio in just two month's time.

When invited by the Chicago branch of the Woman's Christian Temperance Union to be its president, she accepted. Friends warned her against the financial risks, but her mother encouraged her with the words of Psalm 37:3, "Trust in the Lord and do good: So shalt thou dwell in the land and verily thou shalt be fed."

Frances followed this divine pattern for fulfillment by trusting the Lord and living as good a life as possible. She successfully led the Chicago branch into growth and greater effectiveness and after her election as coordinator for the National Woman's Christian Temperance Union, membership soared to one million members! When the World's Woman's Christian Temperance Union was formed, the Union chose Frances Willard as the person most capable of directing its far-reaching activities.

She did not channel all of her boundless energies only into the war against liquor traffic. She soon discovered that people drank to escape the hopelessness of their existence. Saloons looked inviting to laboring men being mistreated in the factories and downtrodden women who were refused even the simple right to vote.

When Frances dared to state these facts publicly, many of her friends and followers gave vocal opposition. "Our business is to keep men sober, not fed," some said. As for woman's suffrage, proposed from the W.C.T.U. platform in 1876 by Frances, it triggered this comment from the chairwoman of the meeting: "The National Woman's Christian Temperance Union is not responsible for the utterances of this evening. We have no mind to trail our skirts in the mire of politics." In a loud, clear voice, Frances courageously retorted, "Then raise your skirts so they won't trail!"

Feeling her health failing, Frances returned to the city where she had begun her teaching career. "When I reach heaven, I want to register as from Evanston," she said, smiling. Later, as death drew near, she whispered, "Other work, in another world."

We can only speculate what her work in the next world might be. We do know, however, that Illinois proudly erected a marble statue of the longtime temperance leader in the Statuary Hall of the Nation's Capital. It is the only woman's statue there.

Although Frances died in 1898, years before Women's Suffrage or Prohibition became law, she died in faith that she had faithfully kept the pledge signed so many years earlier to perpetually hate "all that can intoxicate."

Harriet Ross Tubman

"Moses" of the Nineteenth Century

CHAPTER TWELVE

Although named "Araminta," the woman destined to be remembered for her success as a liberator of slaves, preferred to be called by her mother's name, "Harriet." Later, in appreciation for her unique talents, grateful people admiringly referred to her as "Moses."

Harriet Ross was born around 1820 on a plantation in Dorchester County, Maryland. Her grandparents on both sides had come in chains from Africa. As a young girl, Harriet discovered the agonies of slavery from firsthand experience. Compelled by her masters to work as a maid, a cook, or a field hand, she learned at an early age to produce or face the consequences! When she was thirteen, an overseer struck her head with a two-pound weight and fractured her skull. This injury caused pressure on her brain that would provoke discomfort for the rest of her life. She habitually wore a bandanna to cover the large and ugly scar from this incident.

In 1844, she married a free Negro named John Tubman. Five years later her youthful master died. Harriet heard that his slaves would be sold out of state. She decided to run away and escape to Philadelphia where she found work at a hotel.

The joy of freedom and earning wages did not, however, cause her to forget her people still shackled by slavery. She carefully saved her money so that she could make secret missions into areas still dominated by cruel task masters. In 1850, when Congress passed the Fugitive Slave Act making it a crime to assist runaway slaves, Harriet knew the hour had struck for concerted action.

In December, she made her first mission of mercy. She went to Baltimore, found her sister and two children and helped them to escape. The following year, Harriet did the same for her brother and his family. At a later date, she liberated a group of eleven people which included another brother and his family. In June of 1857, she managed to hire a wagon, put her parents in it and drove them to freedom—perhaps the most unforgettable experience of her action-packed life.

No one knows exactly how many slaves she helped set free. It is believed that she made nineteen trips into Maryland alone during the ten years preceding the Civil War, and may have helped three hundred people to freedom. Sometimes Harriet worked by herself. Other times she worked with people associated with the Underground Railroad and earned herself the reputation of being a "conductor" who never lost a passenger.

Naturally, her success angered those in favor of slavery. At one time, rewards for her capture totaled $40,000. But no one could outwit her strategy. Her tactics would amaze both friend and foe alike. The ideas she came up with were as versatile as they were effective. For example, to alert her people who wished to escape that she was coming, she would send veiled messages such as this one: "Tell my brothers to be always watching unto prayer, and when the good old ship of Zion comes along, to be ready to step on board."

Another time, when Harriet recognized a former master coming her way, she quickly decided that the chickens she had just purchased would create quite a bit of confusion if she let them go. She released them all at once and wildly chased after them. In the mad confusion of dust, feathers and excited reactions, the former master never bothered to see who the woman was!

Harriet also took advantage of the Sunday morning church hour to help her cause. Believing that even the masters had their minds on better things than human oppression during worship time, she led her people to freedom while their masters warmed the church pews.

In April of 1858, Harriet counseled John Brown about his plans to attack slavery by armed action. They met in St. Catharines, Ontario, where Harriet had taken up residence soon after her escape. Brown was so impressed by her spirit and strategy that he nicknamed her "General Tubman."

When the Civil War broke out, Harriet yearned to be of service to her country. Governor John A. Andrew of Massachusetts gave her a printed endorsement. She went to Beaufort, South Carolina, and talked to Major General David Hunter, commander of the Department of the South. He authorized her to serve as a spy and as a scout, tasks which she fulfilled for three years.

When the war ended and the emancipation of her people was assured, Harriet looked around for other ways to help humanity. She opened her farm home near Auburn, New York, to her elderly parents and others, forming the Harriet Tubman Home for Indigent Aged Negroes. This unique haven continued to function for several years even after her death from pneumonia in 1913. When a plaque was erected to her memory in the Auburn town square, the famed Booker T. Washington addressed the crowd that gathered for the occasion.

Years before, Frederick Douglas had written to Harriet, "Excepting John Brown—of sacred memory—I know of no one who was willingly encountered more perils and hardships to serve our enslaved people than you have." No matter what people call her—"Araminta," "Harriet," or "Moses"—by these or any other name this woman is as great!

Martha Washington
America's First Lady
CHAPTER THIRTEEN

Martha Washington, born June 2, 1731, has the distinction of being the First Lady of the new republic. Married at age eighteen to Daniel Custis, she bore four children, two of whom died in infancy. When Daniel died seven years later, he left his young widow a sizeable fortune and two small children to raise.

In 1759, a mutual friend invited George Washington, plantation owner and commander of Virginia forces in the French and Indian War, to meet "the prettiest and richest widow in Virginia" at a private dinner. The couple were immediately attracted to each other.

They met only three more times before they were married in January of the following year. When the courts settled the Custis estate, Martha and her two children Jackie and Patsy came from Williamsburg to Mount Vernon, Washington's 8,000 acre plantation overlooking the famed Potomac River. She immediately assumed full management of the domestic servants and Mount Vernon became known for its warm and gracious hospitality.

The Washingtons' peaceful family life, however, came to an abrupt halt when the colonies decided to break with England. In 1775, Congress chose Washington to command the American forces. That winter, Martha joined her husband at his headquarters in Cambridge, Massachusetts, and later at Valley Forge. She kept cheerful and busy during these long winter months by sewing uniforms for the Revolutionary soldiers.

When her husband became America's First President in 1789, Martha adapted easily to life in New York, the nation's first capital. Then she moved to Philadelphia, the second seat of government. She wrote that she had "learned from experience that the greater part of our happiness or misery depends on our disposition and not on our circumstances."

When Washington refused a third term in office, he and "Lady Washington" joyously returned to their beloved Mount Vernon. She wrote to a friend: "I cannot tell you know much

I enjoy home, after being deprived of one so long, for our dwelling in New York and Philadelphia was not home, only sojourning.... I am fairly settled down to the pleasant duties of an old-fashioned Virginia housekeeper, steady as a clock, busy as a bee and cheerful as a cricket."

In 1802, after a prolonged "severe fever," seventy-one-year-old Martha Washington died and was laid to rest beside her husband in a tomb enclosure he had designed at Mount Vernon. They both had sacrificed much for the success of the new republic. She, like her famed mate, had become "first in war, first in peace" and "first in the hearts" of her countrymen.

Abigail Smith Adams

Wife and Mother of Presidents

CHAPTER FOURTEEN

Martha Washington's successor is remembered for more than just her role as a President's wife. The wife of John Adams, second President of the United States, Abigail was also the mother of John Quincy Adams, America's sixth President. A devoted writer, she developed a spontaneous literary style which established her as the greatest letter writer of her time.

Born on November 11, 1744, in the parsonage of the First Congregational Church of Weymouth, Massachusetts, Abigail felt the godly influence of her parents. Her father, the Reverend William Smith, was the pastor. Her mother, Elizabeth Quincy, was the daughter of Colonel John Quincy, the leading citizen of Braintree.

On October 25, 1764, Abigail married John Adams, who was nine years older. After the ceremony John mounted his horse, swinging his little bride up behind him, went riding to Braintree, Massachusetts, with Abigail's arms around his waist and her scarlet cape flying. With rare tact and judgment Abigail was to counsel her husband through a busy, eventful life. Happily complementing each other's personalities, her serenity of spirit and faith in her lawyer-husband's abilities offset his tendency toward worry and self-depreciation. She was also a monument of faith in God and her country.

During the first decade of their marriage, Abigail gave birth to one daughter and four sons. Her most famous son was John Quincy. In August of 1774, John Adams left for Philadelphia as a delegate to the first Continental Congress. One political assignment followed another and, due in part to the pressures of public service, ten years were to elapse before John and Abigail could be together on a permanent basis again. During this time Abigail bridged their loneliness by letter writing. In 1776, she wrote to her busy husband. "Remember the Ladies, and be more generous and favorable to them than your ancestors.... We will not hold ourselves bound by any laws in which we have no voice, or Representation."

In 1778, Congress sent John to France to negotiate a peace treaty. His oldest son John Quincy accompanied him as personal secretary. Abigail kept the farm in good repair, paid the taxes and bills, kept out of debt, fed and clothed her family. In 1784, John wrote asking Abigail to join him. With her daughter Nabley, she made a rough crossing in the pitching, rolling sea. By the end of the thirty-day voyage she had learned all the nautical terms.

In Paris, Abigail and the Marquise de Lafayette found each other a kindred spirit visiting by the hour over knitting and embroidery, the children at their feet.

Letters from America notified Mr. Adams in May 1785 that he had been appointed first American minister to the Court of St. James in England. Abigail once again demonstrated her tact and skill, playing an important part in the directing of our nation by keeping her husband from losing his temper. She proved a valuable diplomat.

In 1788 Abigail's heart sang when they returned to Braintree.

She maintained the same courageous intelligent spirit during the twelve years (1789-1801) of her husband's vice-presidency and presidency. It was not easy for her as the "First Lady" to move in 1880 into the President's House. A huge, unfinished structure, it was made livable only "by fires in every part, thirteen of which we were obliged to keep daily, or sleep in wet and damp places."

90

After serving his country for twenty-five years, John Adams following his defeat by Thomas Jefferson, decided to retire. He and Abigail returned to their home in Massachusetts. But the next few years were far from quiet ones. The voices of energetic grandchildren punctuated the silence. Their son, John Quincy became more and more popular in the political arena. In 1817, President James Monroe appointed him Secretary of State. Of course, many letters had to be written and who could express herself better than this nineteenth century "Dear Abby"?

Although vibrant, Abigail finally felt the toll the years had taken. In October of 1818, following a case of typhus fever, she died in her sunny, west bedroom in the home she loved and was buried in a crypt under the portico of the First Church of Quincy. Eight years later, John Adams was buried beside her.

The influence of Abigail Smith Adams continued to live on through her distinguished children. John Quincy, who became the sixth President of the United States in 1825, said simply and sincerely, "All that I am, my mother made me."

Juliette Gordon Low

Founder of the Girl Scouts of America

CHAPTER FIFTEEN

Juliette looked in the mirror and frowned. Physically she could compete with other women in their fifties. It wasn't that. The problem lay much deeper, in her emotions. Emptiness and lack of fulfillment showed on her face despite the fact that she should not have had reason to be unhappy.

Juliette was born into an aristocratic family circle in 1860 where luxurious living was the daily life style. She and her sister, Nellie, loved to romp and play games on the grounds surrounding their stately Gordon mansion in Savannah, Georgia.

The years passed. In 1886, Juliette met William Low, a handsome and fascinating Englishman. Born to an American woman, William Low had returned to America to look after some family business interests. He and Juliette married seven months later on December 21, 1886, in a beautiful church wedding.

During the next eighteen years, William and Juliette lived well. They traveled to Europe, Africa and the Orient, socializing with kings, noblemen and such celebrities as Rudyard Kipling, the famous author. They even bought a country estate nestled among the green hills of central England! It seemed the good times would never end for the happy couple. But all to abruptly their good life ended when William became ill and died in 1905.

After his death, Juliette tried to enjoy life as she had known it with William. But the social whirl made her feel more dejected and alone so she began traveling. After a short time, she knew that the change of scenery didn't help and wondered what would restore meaning to her existence.

Slowly a conviction grew in her heart, that she had to find a worthwhile cause to which her life could be devoted, something greater than mere personal enjoyment and comfort.

This feeling intensified in 1911 when she met Sir Robert Baden-Powell. He told her how he had founded the Boy

93

Scouts program and how this growing youth movement kept him active and happy. She listened, complimenting him on his successes and lamenting her failures. "My life has been wasted," she sighed. He replied that she would be guided into the good life, at the right time.

When she asked him why his scouting program seemed to be for boys only, he quickly answered that it was excellent for girls as well. He told her of the English Girl Guide Program. She watched how it was conducted and tried out the theories on a couple of groups she organized herself.

Convinced that America needed such a program, she returned home to Savannah. Gathering eight young girls together on March 12, 1912, she led them in the first Girl Scout meeting held in the United States. As soon as word spread about Juliette's dream, well-meaning friends and relatives warned her of the obstacles.

"Remember, you're fifty-two years old!" one friend cautioned.

Even a nephew came up to her and said, "You have no training in organization, business or finance."

Parents of the girls themselves then started objecting. They didn't like the program of hiking and camping, preferring "more ladylike activities." Sports were for "tomboys" and not for their daughters! Parents in another state observed that the Girl Scout program would make for militarism.

94

Although these criticisms hurt, Juliette did not allow them to stop her. Knowing she loved the girls and that they loved her, she placed their welfare first and allowed little else to matter.

Then, with World War I raging, the tide of public opinion turned in favor of the Girl Scouts of America. Girl Scout troops began knitting sweaters to send overseas to the fighting men. Mrs. Woodrow Wilson, America's First Lady, donned a Girl Scout uniform and endorsed the work of the organization. Later, she invited Juliette and selected scouts to

he White House. Scouting finally received the acceptance it
had so long deserved.

On January 17, 1927, Juliette Gordon Low died in a
Savannah hospital. Few women have been as honored by the
United States government since her death. A World War II
Liberty ship was named for her. In 1948 a postage stamp
carried her picture in Girl Scout uniform. The Gordon Home
in Savannah became the birthplace visited by Scouts who
became childless Juliette Low's heritage.

Amelia Earhart

First Lady of the Air

CHAPTER SIXTEEN

In 1921, after Amelia had crash-landed a small plane in a cabbage patch, her friends wondered if this scare would cause her to change her plans for the future. She replied that this did not dampen her enthusiasm for flying but it did diminish her fondness for cabbage!

Such ready wit and personal warmth were hallmarks of the woman whom newsmen liked to call, "Lady Lindy," associating her with the famed pilot, Charles A. Lindbergh.

Born on July 24, 1897, in Atchison, Kansas, Amelia Mary Earhart soon gained a reputation for liking adventure and being individualistic. Her high school annual had these words under her picture: "Girl in Brown Who Walks Alone."

After her family moved to California, Amelia's individuality surfaced dramatically when she was twenty-three. Taking money intended to buy a dress, she bought a streetcar ticket instead and went to see a stunt-flying exhibition at Glendale, California. After watching the program, she walked up to one of the pilots. Viewing his small, two-seater plane with an open cockpit, she simply said, "I want to go up."

The pilot, surprised, glanced up and noticed the anticipation on her face. "Okay. Let's go!" he answered.

So, with record-holder Frank Hawks, Amelia soared into the wild, blue yonder. Before they had gone three hundred feet into the Air, Amelia knew she had to learn how to fly a plane by herself!

Against her parents' wishes, Amelia began to take flying lessons, supporting herself by working for the telephone company. In June of 1921, she took her first solo flight in a Kinner Airster. She bought her own plane, a Kinner Canary, on her twenty-fifth birthday and used it to set a woman's altitude record of 14,000 feet!

Seven years later, in 1928, she answered the phone and heard a man ask, "Would you like to fly the Atlantic?" She could hardly believe her ears! Was this some jokester?

Little by little she discovered that the offer was indeed authentic. Mrs. Frederick E. Guest, a wealthy Englishwoman born in America, was sponsoring a goodwill flight between the United States and England. Two men, a pilot and a mechanic, would be on board. Mrs. Guest requested that the third person be a woman. Finally, George Putnam, the well-known publisher and his associates chose Amelia because of her flying ability and personal charm. "How could I refuse such a shining adventure?" she said later.

On June 17, 1928, pilot Bill Stultz and mechanic Louis Gordon, with Amelia wedged between the extra gas tanks, took off in the *Friendship* from Newfoundland. Twenty hours and forty minutes later, the plane landed at Burry Port, Wales.

When the news of their success became known, Amelia became an instant celebrity. Although she insisted that she had not flown the plane but had only kept the log and passed the sandwiches, the public believed otherwise about this tall, smiling girl with the tousled blond hair who abstained from both liquor and tobacco.

After ecstatic receptions in England, Amelia returned to her homeland where she was given a ticker-tape parade down Fifth Avenue in New York. She also attended other receptions in her honor in Boston, Chicago and other cities.

Delighted to see that her example opened the minds of other women who had falsely concluded that flying was for men only, putting some of her ideas into book form, she submitted the manuscript to George Putnam. The book was later printed under the title *20 Hours, 10 Minutes.* During their revision of the final copy, something else happened—Amelia and George fell in love. On February 7, 1931, they were married.

Before their marriage, she had made it clear that she wanted to continue her life in the air. Therefore, George wasn't too surprised when one morning, about a year after their marriage, Amelia looked across the breakfast table and asked quietly, "George, would you mind if I flew the Atlantic, alone?" He wisely consented.

On May 21, 1932, Amelia, piloting a Lockheed Vega monoplane, became the first woman to fly the Atlantic alone. The flight, from Harbor Grace, Newfoundland to Culmore, Ireland, took fourteen hours and fifty-six minutes. It also established Amelia as the first person to make the crossing by air more than once. In recognition of her courage, the United States Congress awarded her the Distinguished Flying Cross.

Five years later, while on a round-the-world flight, Amelia and her plane, *The Electra,* disappeared into the Pacific. No trace of Amelia or the plane has ever been found!

In a letter "to be opened in case of death," the spirit of this "Lady Lindy" comes through loud and clear. "Hooray for the last grand adventure!" she wrote. "I wish I had won but it was worthwhile anyway...."

Rachel Carson

Crusader for Conservation

CHAPTER SEVENTEEN

Years before "ecology" became a popular cause for which to crusade, a young woman with a background in genetics, zoology and biology wrote articles and books alerting the public to man's relationship with the living world around him. The prophetic pen belonged to Rachel Carson, whose controversial bestseller *Silent Spring* made her one of the most widely read conservationists of our time.

Born May 27, 1907, in beautiful Springdale, Pennsylvania, Rachel showed her preference for the out-of-doors at an early age. She took great delight in the sights and sounds of the beautiful world God had created. Along with her love of nature came a love for good books. The two loves united years later to make her an eloquent literary crusader for a better environment.

After studying genetics at Johns Hopkins University and graduating with a Master's degree in Zoology, Rachel spent summers studying at the Woods Hole Marine Biological Laboratory in Massachusetts. This training, coupled with experiences in teaching zoology at Johns Hopkins and the University of Maryland, gave her books such as *The Sea Around Us* a ring of authority.

However, it was her exposé of our chemically polluted planet that made Rachel Carson a world figure. Published September 27, 1962, *Silent Spring* challenged the indiscriminate use of chemical insecticides. Cries of protest against that "hysterical woman" came from the chemical industry and the U.S. Department of Agriculture, but Rachel stood her ground. She had researched the entire subject scientifically and had facts and figures to show the terrible effects of some insecticides on birds and fish. She lamented the use of toxic pesticides. Remembering her studies in genetics, she worried about what today's pesticides may be doing to tomorrow's people and pointed out California's records which showed 900 to 1,000 cases of accidental pesticide poisoning per year.

Aware of the public furor over *Silen* Spring, a Science Advisory Committee was commissioned to study the issue and make a report to the public "in a way that will make it aware of the dangers while recognizing the value of pesticides." The pesticides report of the Committee, when finally issued, vindicated the conclusions made in *Silent Spring.*

Rachel felt well repaid for her thorough research now that the federal government and the general public was aware of the pesticide problem. Now direct action could be taken in specific areas of pollution control.

She was never given the chance to act. She grew weaker and died a victim of cancer on April 14, 1964, at the age of fifty-six.

Her great book, however, continues to plead for a healthier, safer environment both for us today and the generations that will follow.

Mary Lyon

Pioneer in Women's Education

CHAPTER EIGHTEEN

The world which Mary Lyon entered on February 28, 1797, was an unfriendly one for the daughters of Eve. Thought to be physically and mentally inferior to men, women were denied entrance to all of the professions and most occupations. Married women could not own property, make contracts, or even lay legal claim to their children. For example, if a husband wanted to give or will his children away, the law supported his action.

Such an unfair, inflexible society might have discouraged most of Mary's contemporaries, but not this human dynamo. When only a toddler, she revealed her ability to cope with any circumstance. Instructed by her mother to accomplish a certain chore in thirty minutes, Mary busied herself but soon found she was running out of time. When twenty-five minutes had gone by, she decided to do something to help ease the situation. She pushed a chair over to the mantlepiece, climbed up, and reversed the hourglass. When her mother asked what she was doing, Mary replied seriously, "I've found a way of making more time."

Along with this ingenuity came a deep personal faith in the Lord and the Bible. Her godly parents, expressing warm love, often took her to the Baptist Meeting House in Ashfield, Massachusetts. Here, not far from her home town of Buckland, she learned of God's great love. On one occasion, she saw several people "under conviction of sin" talking to her grandfather, the Baptist minister. After he had counselled them from the Bible and prayed with them, they left radiating joy and peace. Mary witnessed this dramatic change and felt in her own heart a sense "of God's love and His goodness and of an answering love for Him."

At five, Mary experienced her first sorrow when her father died at the age of forty-four. Some of her resulting loneliness found relief in another experience she had that year. She began attending the little district school about a mile up the road. She loved to learn and worked hard.

In the years that followed, Mary received a rather poor and

irregular education. She longed to attend a quality school. At age nineteen she withdrew her small amount of savings from a hiding place near the fireplace and enrolled in Sanderson Academy, taught by a college graduate.

Mary's brilliant mind soon made the teacher and classmates forget her poorly fitting dress and oversized shoes. Her mental appetite seemed insatiable. She always asked for extra assignments. When her teacher gave her Adam's *Latin Grammar,* he felt it would keep her busy for weeks. He never dreamed that between Friday and Monday she would memorize all the assigned portions and recite the declensions, conjugations and rules of syntax before her teacher and fellow students!

After graduation, she turned to the work she enjoyed most, teaching. When she began teaching at Byfield Academy in Saugus, Massachusetts, she heard the Reverend Joseph Emerson speak. The school's founder, he stated in a dedication message that he believed the day was coming when institutions of learning for women would be regarded as essential as colleges for men. "Where such an institution shall be erected, by whom it shall be founded, is yet for the Hand of Providence to develop," he said. Neither he nor Mary knew that within a few years Providence would select this woman teacher to be one of the most effective pioneers in the field of higher education for women. For the present, however, Mary had other work to do.

106

She resigned from Byfield and returned to her alma mater, Sanderson Academy, to serve as an assistant administrator and its first woman teacher. She had no problem preparing and presenting her lessons. She did, however, have difficulty in keeping order. "I have no natural dignity," she later wrote. When her students got the giggles, so did she. As time passed, she learned greater self-control in the classroom and was able to receive her students' undivided attention. They appreciated her warmth and sense of humor. "God wants you to be happy," she told them. "He made you to be happy."

Mary learned more vital lessons in school administration when she accepted the position as assistant principal at the Adams Female Seminary in Londonderry, New Hampshire. One of her students could recall, fifty years later, "Even now the firm clear tones of her voice echo through my memory, and I see her earnest face, her keen hazel eyes, her auburn hair and strongly marked features the austere simplicity of her dress and the brusque decision in every movement." Truly, Mary Lyon was unforgettable.

After leaving Adams Female Seminary, she joined forces with her close friend Polly Grant, who had started a school in Ipswich, Massachusetts, that dared to try out new concepts. For example, instead of autocratic rule, the students practiced the "honor system." Each young woman reported on her own behavior, such as: "I have kept my chamber in reasonable order"; "I have walked out but once without Miss Farley's apprehension, and with the exception of laughing once at the table, have behaved with propriety."

This daring new school grew and by 1831 only half of the girls who applied could be accommodated. Mary made a mental note that no school could succeed without permanent dormitories and a dining hall. She also made another observation. Schools for women failed because they did not receive sufficient funds. They depended too much on tuition for their survival. Colleges for men, like Harvard and Yale, remained financially solvent year after year because they were endowed. Private gifts paid for the construction of their buildings.

107

Another conviction grew in Mary's heart. Tuition costs had to be lowered if education was to be brought within reach of every woman. She would have to resist the popular opinion that higher education was primarily for the daughters of the rich. The common people had to have "a seminary which would be so moderate in expense as to be open to the daughters of farmers and artisans and to teachers who might be mainly dependent on their own efforts for their support."

Concepts of funding and lower tuition would work, Mary thought, if she could also implement more of what she saw in action during an extensive trip to four states in 1833. In certain "cooperative" schools students shared household tasks, thereby cutting maintenance costs. These schools had proven the practicality of such a plan. If men students could share and share alike, surely women students could do it, and do it better because of their greater experience in domestic work.

Armed with this blueprint for success, Mary called a special meeting at the Ipswich school on September 6, 1834. The vibrant thirty-seven-year-old teacher listed the reasons schools for women fail. Then she shared her plan for a school for women that would not fail. They would build a seminary building to accommodate 175 students, an equipped laboratory and a well-stocked library. A boarding house large enough for 150 residents would be built near by, with rooms to be "finished and furnished so to give ladies as favorable a situation while pursuing their studies as is afforded to young men at our colleges or other seminaries." The construction costs would be financed by endowments from ordinary citizens.

The men present that evening, who would later become "the board of trustees," estimated that $20,000 to $40,000 was needed to begin the construction of this unique school. This was a staggering figure in a day when few shared their enthusiasm for the education of women. Sensing the questions and fears of her friends during the meeting, Mary said confidently, "Faith's business is to make things real." Then she proposed a method which would assure would-be donors that all of their gifts would go directly into the cause of the Seminary and not into fund-raising expenses. The method, still used by fund-raisers today, is to gather an initial sum of money to finance the raising of the main fund. Mary volunteered to raise the initial sum through her efforts among other women.

She set $1,000 as her primary goal. The first $269 came from teachers and pupils at the school where she was acting principal. Then she went from house to house in Ipswich and neighboring communities, asking ladies to share in "the bringing of a liberal education within the means of the daughters of the common people." The housewives gave $475. To raise the remaining amount, she contacted friends and former pupils and wrote scores of letters appealing for investments in the proposed school. Slowly, dollars continued to add up. In less than two months through dedication to her dream, she had met her goal. When it was all over, Mary collapsed from fatigue and was unable to leave her bed for three days.

Aware of the prejudice against women in leadership, she suggested that the board of trustees hire a man to raise the main fund. The Board chose Roswell Hawks, a young minister.

Another of Mary's suggestions accelerated public acceptance of the learning center for women. She believed a school "fitted to a local habitation and a name" would influence public opinion. The board of trustees selected a site at the foot of Mount Holyoke in South Hadley, Massachusetts. Flattered, the townspeople pledged $8,000.

They derived the name "Mount Holyoke Seminary" from the nearby mountain. The word "Seminary" in that day denoted a school of any grade, while the word "college" could have implied a rivalry with male institutions of higher learning.

The efforts of Roswell Hawks produced some funds but the total amount needed to begin construction seemed to be out of reach. Along with the shortage of funds came an abundance of adverse criticism from the public and the news media. Newspaper dubbed Mount Holyoke Seminary "a rib factory," and a "whole-woman-making-school." People said the Seminary was "an innovation uncalled for, unheard of until now since the foundation of the world and unthought of now except by a few strong-minded women and radical men, who would level all distinctions and overturn the foundations of the family, society, the church and the state." Furthermore, the critics declared that the study of mathematics and philosophy "were not suited to the tastes or capacities of women; they didn't want them and wouldn't undertake them; and if they did, they would ruin their health, impair their gentleness, delicacy, modesty and refinement, unsex them and unfit them for their proper sphere." The Seminary also became the butt of a joke about a disgusted farmer who sighs, "They'll be educatin' the cows next." William Seymour Tyler, a professor friend of Mary Lyon, made this summary of the critics' remarks.

Mary Lyon took the criticism in stride, and even firmly and kindly answered the attacks on her person and motives. When accused by a woman of giving in to overwhelming ambition, Mary gently replied, "True humility consists, not in self-depreciation, but in a just estimate of one's own powers or character."

Mary's "just estimate" of herself and her vision underwent further testing. Hawks and the other solicitors reported that the money situation was getting tighter and tighter. "I find it impossible to obtain even a promise of a gift when the times improve," wrote one of the men. Hawks himself worked hard for three months without getting one gift for the Seminary. People sensed that something terrible was about to happen. The next year, America experienced the economic panic of 1837.

Many of the school's supporters suggested the construction plans be postponed until the economy became more stable. The trustees asked Mary to decide whether to wait or not. She asked them for a few days to prayerfully consider the wisest course of action.

She left for Ashfield to visit her mother.

Later, when a neighbor asked what Mary would decide, her mother replied, "Mary will not give up. She just walks the floor and says over and over again, when all is so dark, ' "Commit thy way unto the Lord, trust also in Him, and He shall bring it to pass." Women must be educated—they must!" ' " When her time was up, Mary returned to Ipswich and announced her decision: the construction of the Seminary must go ahead as planned and she would personally go out and solicit the needed funds!

With cheerful determination, she traveled by stagecoach or carriage, telling her story to anyone who would listen. Not everyone would. Some men told her she was too radical. Some women refused to converse. Polite and pleasant to all such people, she would bid them farewell and hurry on to the next house. Generally speaking, though, people listened to her and gave contributions or made pledges.

Some of the gifts represented sacrificial concern. For example, Anne and Lucy Maynard, touched by Mary's appeal, pledged $200 from their meager income. Then, a short time later, fire destroyed their home. The next day, while poking among the ashes, they recovered several silver dollars—dollars they had saved to help meet their pledge for Mount Holyoke. When they finally sent in their $200, after long hours of sewing and weaving, they enclosed the darkened coins. Knowing the sacrifice the coins represented, Mary insisted they be kept as souvenirs to remind people in years to come of the love and dedication that helped to make the Seminary a reality. She then used her own money to make up the difference caused by her decision to keep the darkened coins as reminders of Anne and Mary's beautiful faith in higher education for women.

111

Although she made most of her appeals to individuals, she welcomed opportunities to speak to groups at district schoolhouses and village churches. "Mount Holyoke will light a torch which will gleam throughout the world and it depends upon you and upon me," she would declare enthusiastically. "Don't think any gift too small. I want the twenties and the fifties, but the dollars and half dollars, with prayer, go a great way. We have to have prayer in the new school, so let it be gifts with prayer."

Mary's combined faith and persistence achieved the financial goal which seemed to be an impossibility a year or two before. The figures were most encouraging: 1,800 persons in ninety-two communities had given cash or made pledges totaling $27,000, two thousand dollars more than the amount which the trustees had said should be secured before construction could begin.

As the five-story building began taking shape, an ecstatic Mary Lyon exclaimed, "The stones and brick and mortar speak a language which vibrates through my very soul!" The conviction continued and on November 8, 1837, Mount Holyoke Female Seminary opened its doors. Eighty young ladies formed the original student body. This figure rose to 116 before the first year came to a close. Students came from New England, New York, Pennsylvania, New Jersey and even Ohio.

The following August 23rd, white-gowned students followed School Principal Mary Lyon to the village church for the first commencement. There, three seniors received their graduation certificates. "It was an hour in her life never to be forgotten," observed an associate of Mary's. "The battle had been fought, the victory was hers...."

112   For twelve years, she continued to guide the Seminary in its goals and in its growth. Gradually, it reached the proportions she had envisioned and began to compare favorably with the famed men's colleges in New England. More important, she received grateful letters from alumni, many of whom had become foreign missionaries. Her prediction had come true—Mount Holyoke had lit a torch "which will gleam throughout the world."

In 1849, weakened by influenza, she contracted erysipelas from one of her students whom she had tried to help during her fatal illness. She died on March 5 at the age of fifty-two and went to be with the Lord she had loved and served since childhood. Her body was laid to rest at the foot of an oak tree on a slope east of the original building at Mount Holyoke. On the tombstone was inscribed: "Founder of Mount Holyoke Female Seminary, a teacher for thirty-five years of more than three thousand pupils...." Then the lettering shares her philosophy of life: "There is nothing in the universe that I fear, but that I shall not know all my duty, or shall fail to do it."

Henrietta Mears
Vibrant Teacher of God's Word

CHAPTER NINETEEN

Henrietta, there's something I must tell you," the doctor said kindly. "You are losing your sight." He paused and looked sympathetically at his youthful, intelligent patient who had high hopes for her first year at the University of Minnesota. "I must warn you that unless you discontinue reading and studying, blindness is imminent." Then, reaching for a glimmer of hope, he added, "It is possible that you may be able to conserve the eyesight you have remaining if you do as I have suggested."

As Henrietta Mears left his office, mixed emotions raced through her heart and mind. Could anything be worse than the prospect of physical blindness, to never see the faces of family members and friends or thrill to the splendor of a sunset? Maybe she could no longer even have a quiet evening in the company of a book! Yet the alternative of mental blindness distressed her even more. How could she forfeit her education and give up her plans to be a successful teacher? How could she live without learning?

She remembered the way her thirst for knowledge became evident as a child. After only one day in kindergarten, she told her beloved mother, "Kindergarten is to 'muse little children and I'se 'mused enough. I want to be 'edicated."

Could she now abandon this dream?

Never indecisive, she expressed her feelings in these words spoken to her mother: "If I am going to be blind by thirty, then blind I shall be! But I want something in my brain to think about!"

Henrietta enrolled for her freshman year with a carefully planned strategy. She would study by daylight, listen intently during lectures and master a book in one reading. By maximum use of her ears and mind and minimum use of her eyes, she finished her freshman year successfully.

She continued this disciplined method of study year after year, graduating with excellent grades and her eyesight intact!

Following graduation, Henrietta entered the teaching field

with enthusiasm and determination. She carefully prepared and skillfully presented her lessons. Her students returned the love she reflected in and out of the classroom.

During this time, she did not forget her Christian faith which had always been dear to her. No matter how busy she became, she stayed involved in a local Sunday School, continuing this service even while a teacher and principal at the same time!

Born in Fargo, North Dakota, on October 23, 1890, Henrietta grew up in a family that actively followed Jesus Christ. At her birth, her father is said to have exclaimed, "Praise God, it's a girl! I couldn't face rearing another son!" However, as the years passed, her father discovered that girls can be as trying as boys. Henrietta shared her brothers' zest for living and wanted to be involved in the action. But she also shared her mother's practice of prayer.

As a toddler she had noticed that every morning her mother entered a certain room, got down on her knees, folded her hands and moved her lips. With typical childish imitation, Henrietta soon knelt next to her mother, folded her chubby little hands and moving her bright red lips. Pleased, Mrs. Mears put her arm around her daughter and explained that she was talking to the God up in heaven who loved everyone and who would hear Henrietta when she prayed. Responding to this loving God at the age of five, Henrietta invited God's Son, Jesus Christ, into her heart to be her personal Savior.

These important childhood memories lingered as she became older. Sunday School provided many opportunities to share her experiences with young and old, many of whom were not blessed with the godly background Henrietta had enjoyed.

Such a vivacious young teacher did not go unnoticed by the young men of the community. The only man, however, whom Henrietta felt she could love in return had chosen a different religious faith. Tall and handsome, he tried to

116

ersuade her that they could each follow their own religious convictions separately, even in marriage. She knew differently. It was as impossible as a home where at mealtime the husband would eat in the dining room and the wife would eat in the kitchen! Strengthened by the Lord, she terminated the friendship and remained single to serve Him wherever He might lead.

As she made this difficult decision, she had no way of knowing that God had reserved for her a satisfying and worldwide ministry based in California. Like many great happenings, God's plan in her life began with a simple gesture of Christian hospitality. Henrietta and her sister Margaret invited the guest preacher at their church to join them for Sunday dinner. Dr. Steward P. MacLellan, pastor of the First Presbyterian Church of Hollywood, California, enjoyed their savory meal and delightful conversation and made them promise to return his visit if they ever traveled to California.

At the time, the two sisters thought a trip to California would be an impractical dream. All their family, friends and interests centered in Minnesota. What would ever draw them to the West Coast?

A few years later, circumstances changed. Henrietta had to decide how and where to spend her sabbatical year. At last both sisters made plans to take an extensive tour of Europe, a trip which promised to be interest-packed and educational.

When they returned to the United States, Henrietta still had some time left on her sabbatical. Deciding California would be a good place to spend the winter months, they left immediately for the Golden State and looked up Dr. Mac Lellan.

Dr. "Mac" showed them his growing church near the famed corner of Hollywood and Vine in Hollywood. They learned that originally it had been a small country church but that under God's blessing the church had grown into one of the nation's most influential Presbyterian churches.

117

During their visit, the pastor gave Henrietta several opportunities to address various groups. Each time the audience responded warmly to her and to her vision of reaching people for Jesus Christ. Deeply impressed, Dr. "Mac" asked the Minnesota school teacher if she would come to Hollywood and be their Director of Christian Education. Fully aware that if she moved she would have to leave old friends and familiar places and give up the security of her teaching contract, she promised to pray for God's will in the matter.

After an interesting series of events, Henrietta knew without a doubt that she belonged in the field of Christian education. Hollywood was her mission field, so she and Margaret moved west.

Right from the start, God gave Henrietta unusual wisdom in leading and motivating the people with whom she came in contact. "I believe I know just what you are thinking," she said kindly to the people attending the first teachers' and officers' meeting. "I think I might feel the same way if I were in your place. 'Another director of the Sunday School—new plans, new ideas, her way of doing things! So everything is going to be changed again! If I have to reorganize my class once more, or try out some fancy new theory, I'll just die! What does she know about Hollywood, anyway?'" Her audience laughed at her accurate diagnosis.

118

"You don't like change and neither do I," she continued. "... So here is what I thought we might do. We'll all relax for six months and use the time for observation. Then we'll sit down and evaluate the situation and decide together what we need to do. You undoubtedly will have some ideas and I might just possibly have a suggestion or two myself!"

Needless to say, this light, warm approach won the cooperation of her staff. No one wanted to wait six months. Teachers called for Henrietta's help and suggestions immediately.

The new Director of Christian Education had to overcome

large problem with the youth of the church. "I don't wanna go to Sunday School anymore," one boy stated bluntly. "All they do is tell you the same old story over and over and over again, only it just gets dumber and dumber." To overcome this lack of interest, Henrietta and her associates began writing their own Sunday School lessons. These were so interesting, Scriptural and practical that parents and their children would come from miles around. The Sunday School program grew tremendously.

As time passed, leaders and teachers from other churches asked if they could purchase these lessons for their Sunday Schools. At first, Henrietta shook her head. Mimeographed lessons just didn't look saleable and were written for just one church situation. Would they be acceptable in all churches? After much prayer she made the decision to print the lessons making them available to all churches and denominations. Thus one of today's successful publishing companies, Gospel Light Publications of Glendale, California began its operations.

Publishing and leading did not dull Henrietta's desire to teach. In fact, she is best remembered as a vibrant Bible teacher. When she spoke, her words had authority and commanded undivided attention. Her biblical, logical and informative lessons challenged each student to accept the claims of Christ on his life.

119

Henrietta delighted in teaching Romans, the sixth book of the New Testament. She loved to emphasize that no one can deliberately earn God's favor. Only through faith in the living Christ, she taught, can one be justified before God.

"I may not be able to answer all students' questions and doubts," she told concerned teachers, "but I can introduce them to the One who can." She thus spent much of her time and ministry introducing people to Christ on a person-to-person basis. "If you want to fill a dozen milk bottles, you must not stand back and spray at them with a hose. You may get them wet, but you won't fill them. You must take them one by one."

As much as Henrietta loved to lead people to Christ, she was not content until the new converts received follow-up instruction. Through "discipling," these men and women grew in grace and in the knowledge of Jesus Christ and became trained to be leaders in the work of the Lord. "Leadership begins with Christ," she said emphatically. "No matter how brilliant a youth may be, he must experience the regenerating power of the resurrected Christ before his real potential can be liberated."

Many of today's Christian leaders felt the influence of this devoted teacher. For example, she took a deep, personal interest in the life and ministry of Bill Bright, the leader of Campus Crusade for Christ. Dr. Billy Graham often telephoned her for advice. At Forest Home, a conference center Henrietta founded, Dr. Graham won victory over a spiritual battle just before his memorable Los Angeles Crusade in 1949. Dr. Graham has described Henrietta Mears as "one of the greatest Christians I have ever known."

In addition to teaching, publishing, leading and counseling, she helped start the Hollywood Christian Group. This group, meeting in Henrietta's spacious Bel Aire home, ministered to actors, actresses and other people of the movie world. Giving celebrities the opportunity to share the truths of God's Word without the spotlight of publicity and the stares of the curious, many famous people encountered Christ.

Another outreach, called GLINT, Gospel Literature in National Tongues, was organized in 1961 to provide Christ-centered Sunday School literature for the mission fields of the world. Henrietta realized the need for such a ministry as she traveled around the world and saw children and college students avidly reading Communist literature. She concluded, "... By God's grace, I must do something," and GLINT came into being.

Two years later at age seventy-two, Henrietta sensed that death was approaching. Her ministries were flourishing, but he had an awareness that "I won't be here next year."

As she looked back on the way God had led her, gratitude welled up in her soul. He had used her beyond her fondest hopes. He had spared her eyesight although she had battled extreme myopia and general eye weakness all her life. "I believe my greatest spiritual asset throughout my entire life has been my failing sight," she said, "for it has kept me absolutely dependent upon God."

She faced death as she had faced life, with confident anticipation. "If you ever happen to see in the obituary column that Henrietta Mears has died," she once said, "don't you believe it! This old body may die, but I'll be glad of that. I wouldn't want to have to go through eternity with this deteriorating one. I'll have a new body...."

On March 20, 1973, "Teacher" left the classroom of time for her sabbatical in eternity. Nearly two thousand people, hundreds of whom Henrietta had personally led to Christ, filed silently into the First Presbyterian Church of Hollywood to honor the memory of their teacher, friend, and leader.

After tributes and messages, the triumphant memorial service came to a close with the choir singing Handel's majestic "Hallelujah Chorus." The great crowd stood to its feet, this time not in honor of their deceased teacher but in worship to their Living Savior. When the mighty anthem ended, a man whispered to his neighbor, "Dear Teacher! Even in her death she pointed us to Christ." Could any greater tribute be given a teacher of God's Word?

The Statue of Liberty

A Final American Woman to Remember ...

CHAPTER TWENTY

A proud woman stands on Liberty Island in New York Harbor. Her loose robe falls in graceful folds to the top of the pedestal on which she stands. In her right arm is a great torch, held high in the air. In her left arm, a tablet bears the date of the Declaration of Independence. On her head sits a crown with ray-like spikes. At her feet lies a broken shackle, symbolizing the defeat of tyranny.

Although her proper name is "Liberty Enlightening the World," friends call her by her popular name, "The Statue of Liberty."

Since the day in 1884 when France gave her to the United States, she has stood as a symbol of American liberty. Immigrants have felt safe and secure at the sight of her welcome.

A woman named Emma Lazarus expressed the feelings well in a poem titled "The New Colossus." The lines of this poem were inscribed on a tablet in the pedestal of the Statue of Liberty in 1903.

"Not like the brazen giant of Greek fame,
With conquering limbs astride from land to land;
Here at our sea-washed, sunset gates shall stand
A mighty woman with a torch, whose flame
Is the imprisoned lightning, and her name
Mother of Exiles. From her beacon-hand
Glows world-wide welcome; her mild eyes command
The air-bridged harbor that twin cities frame.
'Keep ancient lands, your storied pomp!' cries she
With silent lips.

'Give me your tired, your poor,
Your huddled masses yearning to breathe free,
The wretched refuse of your teeming shore.
Send these, the homeless, tempest-tost to me,
I lift my lamp beside the golden door!' "